A Nation

Pierced

Norman Ramsey

The Colors of Grace Publishing Company, Inc.

A Nation Pierced:

A Call to a Nation under Judgment

The Colors of Grace

Publishing Company

The version of scripture used throughout the book is the New International Version (NIV) unless otherwise noted.

Acknowledgements

First, I give thanks to God for being faithful and true and acknowledge the Spirit of Jesus is the spirit of prophecy. I thank God for speaking to his servants in the last days and for giving dreams and visions that remind us of what He has already spoken. I also have to thank God for the revelation of the pathway of grace and for the clarity it has brought to my life.

I am thankful for the congregations with which I have served over the years. For this book in particular, I have been helped by the Sunday Night Bible Study group at Laurel Hill United Methodist Church who encouraged me greatly while I was writing this book. We were studying sin and *The Path of the Blind* when I began this writing and *Conquering the Game of Control* by Dr. Craig Green when I finished. The hope I carried through these times of study sustained me in writing some of the hard things that needed to be said here. Thank you to the Norman Ramsey Ministries' Board of Directors for their support; for Gerald Bowles in particular for being such a solid friend and for giving your honest reaction to all I write. A special acknowledgment goes to my niece Carrie Bailey who created the cover art for this project.

Thank you, to my wife Karen, for not complaining when I get up at 4:00am to go write and for the loving way you have borne all the ways I feel compelled to express what is in my heart. Thanks to my children and grandchildren for living and enjoying the grace that God gives to you in Jesus Christ.

> "Humble yourselves, therefore, under God's mighty hand, that he may lift you up in due time. Cast all your anxiety on him because he cares for you. Be self-controlled and alert. Your enemy the devil prowls around like a roaring lion looking for someone to devour. Resist him, standing firm in the faith, because you know that your brothers throughout the world are undergoing the same kind of sufferings. And the God of all grace, who called you to his eternal glory in Christ, after you have suffered a little while, will himself restore you and make you strong, firm and steadfast. To him be the power for ever and ever. Amen. (I Peter 5: 6 – 11)

About the Author

Norman Ramsey is a unique pastor, performer, author, and songwriter. His desire to make the grace and joy of Jesus as unavoidable as possible has led him to minister throughout the United States, Brazil, Kenya and Honduras. He is founder and president of Norman Ramsey Ministries, Inc. and serves as a United Methodist pastor. Norman is the author of *Moving at the Speed of Grace: Discovering the Way God Works* and *More than Breathing: Pursuing Life in the Power of the Spirit*. Norman has three musical recordings: *Near to the Heart of God*, *Apprentice*, and *The Colors of Grace*.

NY Times Bestselling author and syndicated radio host Dave Ramsey described Norman's ministry as "incredible", going on to say that "his mixing of song, wisdom, and humor really had an impact". Norman and his wife Karen have four, adopted children and live in Virginia.

If you want to find out more about Norman Ramsey Ministries, go to http://normanramsey.com or join us on Facebook at Norman Ramsey Ministries or follow us @normanramsey on Twitter and discover how you can have an unavoidable experience of the grace and joy of Jesus every single day!

Table of Contents

Introduction: The Dream

"I have a dream." Martin Luther King, Jr. August 28, 1963

"I, Daniel, was the only one who saw the vision; the men with me did not see it, but such terror overwhelmed them that they fled and hid themselves." (Daniel 10: 7)

"Jesus went through all the towns and villages, teaching in their synagogues, preaching the good news of the kingdom and healing every disease and sickness. When he saw the crowds, he had compassion on them, because they were harassed and helpless, like sheep without a shepherd. Then he said to his disciples, 'The harvest is plentiful but the workers are few. Ask the Lord of the harvest, therefore, to send out workers into his harvest field'." (Matthew 9: 35 – 38)

It wasn't the first dream I had ever had. It was the first and only dream I ever had with a date: 6/22, June 22nd. Something significant was going to happen that day; something that would forever change the landscape of the world in which we live.

Japan

The dream began with an earthquake in Japan. The devastation was widespread and came from the after effects and tsunami more than the actual earthquake. I asked God why and I heard him say, "Because they honor their dead more than they honor me, the Living God.

The United States

The centerpiece of the dream was California and the earthquake that shook them down to their core. Unlike Japan, in the United States the devastation was wrought by the earthquake itself. It was a terrible shaking unlike any other before it. I asked God, "Why?" God said it was because, "They think they are so substantial but I will shake them and show them they are hollow like a drum. They say they are great and they make great noise about themselves but they are empty."

The Last Thing Before I Woke Up

There was going to be a plane crash in Eastern Europe. Mikhail Gorbachev was on the plane. The plane is shrouded in clouds and storm but it is going down right before I awaken. I ask God, "What about us?" The dream had skipped from the western United States to this event in Europe. God simply said, "I will deal with you in another way."

After waking from the dream, I asked friends what I should do. I believe this had been a revelation that I should share but all of my friends said to wait, seal up the revelation until it could be measured against what was taking place in the world. So, that's what I did. I made a copy for myself and a friend and sent these copies through the postal service so we would have it date stamped.

I am writing to you what I remember of the dream. The letters themselves are still sealed up but I am writing because of events that are unfolding before us. Two things prompted me to revive the dream and put it on paper. One event was the release in 2012 of James Robison's and Jay Richard's book *Indivisible: Restoring Faith, Family, and Freedom Before It's Too Late*. It's warning to restore godly foundations before it's too late prompted me to issue this call of repentance to a nation that is pierced by its own transgressions; even though the good news found in the scripture tells us Jesus has already withstood the cross and been pierced for us. (John 19: 33 – 37)

The second reason, I write now is we may have already seen the partial fulfillment of the dream. On March 11th, 2011, my wife Karen awoke me from sleep at 4:30am. She had been restless and had gotten up that morning, turned on the television, and witnessed the scenes from Japan's earthquake. Usually, I have to check the calendar to know the date of any given day, but when she woke me up and told me the news my first thought was *we are exactly halfway to the date of the dream*.

On March 11, 2013, another earthquake made headlines. I read the International Business Times article where Roxanne Palmer shared words from Pat Abbott, a professor emeritus of geology at San Diego State University, who "warned residents to be on the lookout in an interview with a San Diego NBC affiliate. 'There's always that slight chance – slight chance now - that this could be the foreshock of something larger. Probably not. Usually this is just an event all by itself,' Abbott told NBC." I pray he is right. I do not know if this will be the year of the dream's fulfillment. What I do know, the words "could be the foreshock of something larger" running through my mind, is I must share the dream and share its prophetic consequences.

The prophetic words of Jesus meant to lead us to repentance remind us the last sign of God beginning his final judgment is "earthquakes in various places". (Matthew 24: 7) The shaking revealed in my dream may be the echo and reverberation of God's last call to us as a nation pierced.

This is why I write this book. I am holding out hope for the USA but only if we will repent. For all of us for whom life is an unsolvable puzzle, we must return Jesus to the front of the box and quit the abstract of ourselves we've been using the pieces of our lives to construct. I am asking God to speak to us as a nation pierced and that we will listen.

Prophecy is meant to accomplish three things: reveal something about Jesus Christ, move us to repentance and worship, and reinforce and repeat the work of the Holy Spirit. (John 16: 7 – 15) As those three things are done the Apostle Paul says we will be strengthened, encouraged, and comforted. (1 Corinthians 14: 3) I pray the words of this book will do all three in you.

A House Divided

"A house divided against itself cannot stand...I do not expect the Union to be dissolved — I do not expect the house to fall — but I do expect it will cease to be divided. It will become all one thing or all the other."
(Abraham Lincoln, June 17, 1858)

"If a kingdom is divided against itself, that kingdom cannot stand."
(Jesus the Christ, Mark 3: 24)

We are a house divided. It is obvious. We are divided by age and philosophies of life. We are divided by racial tensions and mistrust among people groups. We are divided by our manners of communication. We are divided by faith and unbelief. We are divided by opportunities for productivity and enslavement to rules and regulations that debase our freedom. We are divided by abilities to reason and the lawlessness that arises when there is a lack of reason.

We are divided by lies and cover ups. We are divided by party politics. We are divided between those who are greedy for profit or privilege and those who are content and at peace with the fruit of their labor.

What happens to a house divided? It cannot stand and it is destined to fall. But is it a foregone conclusion that a fall will occur? Can there be hope for a recovery?

I don't know. When I was a teenager I went through a season where my blood pressure and my blood sugar decided to see how low they could go. I and my father, who had a similar struggle with low blood pressure at the time, would joke about who had the family record. I don't remember who won. One of us had a systolic and diastolic reading of 42 over 30, the other 40 over 32. We felt like two dead men walking. Anytime I closed my eyes and I wasn't lying down, I soon would be.

The first time I discovered this nugget of information I was standing in a little country church where the quartet I sang in during high school was the special music for a revival. We were all standing in the front of the church when the preacher said, "Let's bow our heads for the benediction." I closed my eyes and the next thing I know my friend, Richard Boaz is holding me and keeping me from hitting the floor. With my eyes open, he helped me get upright before the preacher finished what he was saying.

I just wasn't thinking about it the next time it happened. I closed my eyes because the preacher said, "Let us pray." One second I was sitting on the back row of the choir of my home church, the next second I was slamming my head into the pew in front of us. Daddy was mad because I was making noise during the prayer. I almost fell over at the end of that service during the benediction but opened my eyes almost as soon as I had closed them. The good news is I changed my diet, fixed what was wrong, and have never had that problem again.

Can we do the same thing as a country? Can we come to a place of change? Can we fix what is wrong so that we do not experience the problems in the same way again? Do we have a friend or ally who can catch us as we fall and return us to uprightness? I am sorry to say, I do not believe it is possible in the present moment to find a friend or a solution to what ails us.

You see, the path towards repentance begins in traveling the pathway of sin in reverse. We have to own or take responsibility for where we are to move to where we need to be. Let's look at the pathway of sin. It is not hard to comprehend since it has been the same since the beginning. I'll lay it out and then we'll talk about what has to happen for us to operate under grace instead of sin, to constitute our society so that it produces life and liberty instead of death and destruction.

The pathway of sin begins in betrayal as we miss the mark for which we or any given moment is created. This betrayal or falling short locks us into a self-serving bias. We live in a box of our own perceptions and when those perceptions cannot be altered on the way back to repentance we move into blame. Blame by its nature does not take the responsibility necessary for turning around or admitting a bias so inevitably it moves to bitterness. Bitterness locks us into acting out of necessity the way we do. If something has to give, bitterness gives way to bloodshed. Bloodshed ushers us towards a breaking point of judgment and the bondage of repetition.

Each step along this pathway carries a shadow over it that obscures our chances of turning to the truth and keeps us blinded and veiled to other choices that are available to us. The shadow that lies over our betrayal is the shadow of deceit. No person or nation has ever fallen because it obeyed the truth. Our fall as in the beginning starts with believing and obeying a lie.

The shadow that hovers over our bias is the shadow of doubt. What about the proud who hold no doubts but are strong in their own stubbornness? They have to live doubting everyone but themselves. They may boast of a grand vision but it only extends to those who can fall in lockstep with them.

The shadow that shelters our blame is the shadow of division and debt. Our bitterness is shadowed by despair. The shadow of death lurks waiting over our bloodshed and the shadow of destruction raises its ugly head over the breaking points of our lives.

All of these shadows can be dispelled. All of them have to give way to the light of grace that begins in repentance. There is no step down the path of sin that cannot be redeemed by the regeneration of life that begins in repentance as we follow the pathway of grace. This place of beginning again draws us into a believing way of faith where we exchange the bias of our sin for the word and way of God. We build up our faith taking responsibility for our lives through prayer and service. We bless others and are free to do anything we need to do- empowered by the Holy Spirit.

We bring life in the name of Jesus. If something has to give, we join him in the suffering and passion of the cross. We are moving towards a breakthrough into newness of life. The Resurrected Lord moves us forward!

Again, sin always begins in betrayal as we "fall short of the glory of God". (Romans 3: 23) It locks us into a self-serving biased way of doing things. Barring repentance, it moves on to blame. Blame carries us to a bitter place where we become even more acclimated to justifying ourselves in all we have to do. Something has to give and bloodshed occurs and the breaking point of judgment follows.

Reconciliation does not come naturally. The apostle Paul calls it a ministry or service. (2 Corinthians 5: 18) It does not come inevitably like a pendulum's swing returning from where it has swung. Isaiah the prophet says, "But your iniquities have separated you from your God; your sins have hidden his face from you, so he will not hear." (Isaiah 59: 2) Sin has unhinged us from what is first and above all so there must be a reconnect.

Reconciliation and restoration are work, much harder than blaming others or scapegoating ourselves. It can be tedious and humiliating especially when our ways have created problems that are drawing near to becoming insurmountable.

We see it when we recognize where we are as a nation. We live under the shadow of division and debt. We constantly blame others for the inefficiency and unsustainability of our own ideas. Our leaders have written laws to paper over the ditches and graves their actions have dug. Even if we begin to move in the direction of repentance, we must wade back through the bias that has caused us to distrust and be suspicious of one another. We will have to forsake our ideologies, admitting that our way was a betrayal of the truth.

Reality will drive us one way or the other. Either we will do the hard work that leads us to repentance or we will slide into despair. Signs are available that point both directions. Some held out hope that the elections of 2012 would make a difference. But, that event has come and gone and no fundamental change in our division has occurred.

Will the election of a man, republican or democrat, be the solution to what ails us and divides us? No, we have every reason to believe that unless we repent every election will be wielded as a wedge that further divides our country.

Have we come to the place of irreconcilable differences? Signs of blood: murders, bounties, threats, and regulations that force us to act against our conscience forecast the storm that destroys has already been spotted on the horizon. We have only one way of sheltering ourselves from the wrath that is to come and that is through repentance and seeking mercy rather than justice.

We have conveniently tried to walk on the pathway of grace while being rooted to the pathway of sin. We can fool ourselves for a time thinking we can multi-task and walk under the shadow of sin while declaring we are walking in the light. But, our sins have a way of finding us out. R. G. Lee's classic sermon from 1 Kings 21, *Payday Someday* says "The retributive providence of God is a reality as certainly as the laws of gravitation are a reality. And to Ahab and Jezebel, payday came as certainly as night follows day, because sin carries in itself the seed of its own fatal penalty." (http://www.newsforchristians.com/clser1/lee-rg001.html Payday Someday by Robert G. Lee)

Are we in America already carrying "the seed of our own fatal penalty"? Can we come to a national place of humility and repentance and ask God to excise this fatal seed from within us?

I pray we can recognize there is a great deal of difference between the humble way of love and compassion that moves someone to be helpful to another and the proud way of concern that coerces and forces one group to be obligated to serve the needs of another group. Jesus said your neighbor is the one who shows mercy. We have changed the story of the Good Samaritan and turned it on its head. Good Samaritans are no longer permissible by law.

Imagine how the story Jesus told would play out now. A man was going down from Washington D. C. to Richmond, Virginia when he fell into the hands of robbers. They stripped him of his clothes, beat him and went away, leaving him half dead. A priest happened to be going down the same road, and when he saw the man, he passed by on the other side. So too, a lawyer, when he came to the place and saw him, called 911 and then passed by on the other side. But a rich man, as he traveled, came where the man was; and when he saw him, he took pity on him. He went to him and bandaged his wounds, pouring on oil and wine. Then he put the man in his vehicle, took him to an inn and took care of him. The next day he took out twenty thousand dollars and gave them to the innkeeper. "Look after him," he said, "and when I return, I will reimburse you for any extra expense you may have".

Meanwhile, the local emergency management dispatcher that received the 911 call sent an ambulance and state highway patrol to the scene. When they arrived on scene, no one was there, yet both the paramedics and the patrolman identified evidence consistent with what had been reported on the 911 call. A manhunt was initiated and the FBI was called into assist local homicide with the investigation. An APB and an arrest warrant were issued for the person or persons responsible for disturbing the crime scene and for removing the body. The next morning, the local innkeeper saw the report on the news and called police. They came and transported the recovering victim to the hospital. The 'Good Samaritan' was arrested later that day for kidnapping, practicing medicine without a license, and failure to report a crime. The twenty thousand dollars given to the innkeeper for medical expenses was seized as evidence.

The innkeeper was charged with aiding in the committing of a felony and was later fined for allowing his inn to be used as a hospice in clear violation of the zoning permit for its business. The prosecutor argued successfully that the innkeeper and not the county hospital should be responsible for the victim's medical costs since the state provided for the road by which the inn received its business. All costs associated with the investigation and hospitalization would be garnished from the profits of the inn. The rich, 'Good Samaritan' was sentenced to 1,000 hours approved community service and received a suspended sentence of eight years and fined $2,000,000 plus court costs. The $20,000 left to the innkeeper was also kept for court costs.

Due to the designation as a crime scene and the publicity of the trial, the inn went out of business and the innkeeper declared bankruptcy. The hospital after much legal wrangling was paid by the county. The no longer rich, 'Good Samaritan' completed his required community service, and never helped anyone again.

There is only one remedy left to us. Become one of God's people again. Become a person who is called by his name. Some fear a theocracy; that is not for what I am calling. I am calling each of us to allow our character to be reformed so we reflect the spirit of Jesus Christ. I am calling for a revival of scriptural holiness throughout the land.

Every nation has an identity, an esprit de corps, "a common spirit of comradeship, enthusiasm, and devotion to a cause among the members of a group." Once that is lost, we become a balkanized, alienated conglomeration of diverse groups. We are no longer naturally cooperative but ask for a greater governing authority than love to supervise others so we don't get ripped off or taken advantage of. We become a house divided. We cannot live and let live. Someone might succeed beyond me. Someone might be greedy or unfair. The sad truth is we call for laws that enforce upon others what we do or wish to do ourselves.

There are two ways ahead for us as a nation: humility or tyranny, humility or austerity. Humility will allow us to remain a civil society. Corporations and individuals must be shown that the fruit of immoral behavior will eventually perish. Punishment not bailouts must be the expected result of mismanagement and wrongdoing. Only what is godly and lovely will abide the test of time. Austerity alone will lead to anger and depression. We must come to a place of repentance as a nation or we will be lost. What is repentance? It is an alignment of our life and ways with the God of creation and redemption. We must turn to walk with God. No election can save us because no man can save us, regardless of party or popularity. Our hope as *united* states of America begins with our reconciliation to God through Jesus the Christ.

Study Questions:

1. Do you believe we are a nation divided? If so, what divides us and what has kept us from falling apart?

2. What gives you hope that our divisions can be mended and overcome?

3. Has the "seed of our own fatal penalty" germinated and begun to blossom? Is it bearing bad fruit? What would it look like for our nation to experience a spiritual seed transplant surgery where the "seed of our own fatal penalty" is replaced by the "imperishable seed" of God's word?

4. Do you agree with Norman that austerity alone will not restore our nation to good standing? Why or why not?

5. Can you describe another means of salvation for our nation other than Jesus Christ? Can you imagine and articulate how being reconciled to God in Jesus Christ would accomplish that goal?

Signs of the Times

Jesus left the temple and was walking away when his disciples came up to
him to call his attention to its buildings. "Do you see all these things?" he
asked. "I tell you the truth, not one stone here will be left on another;
every one will be thrown down." As Jesus was sitting on the Mount of
Olives, the disciples came to him privately. "Tell us," they said, "when will
this happen, and what will be the sign of your coming and of the end of
the age?" Jesus answered: "Watch out that no one deceives you. For
many will come in my name, claiming, 'I am the Christ,' and will deceive
many. You will hear of wars and rumors of wars, but see to it that you are
not alarmed. Such things must happen, but the end is still to come. Nation
will rise against nation, and kingdom against kingdom. There will be
famines and earthquakes in various places. All these are the beginning of
birth pains."

(Matthew 24: 1 - 8)

There is an urgency underpinning our days unlike any other. It is created
by the all-encompassing Love of God preparing to come in glory and
power. The King of kings is drawing near. "For as lightning that comes
from the east is visible even in the west, so will be the coming of the Son
of Man." (Matthew 24: 27) This urgency is also produced by the
judgments and turmoil that will be roiled up in advance of His coming.
Like billowing clouds on the horizon, there is always a herald or evidence
when something great is coming your way.

Jesus shares some of these signs in Matthew 24. These signs follow the
pathway of God's gracious way of working in our lives. As you observe

these signs that mark our times, I pray you will humbly and quickly put your affairs in order. I pray you will not be a house divided against yourself. You cannot stand in the days ahead if you are.

Prepare the way of the Lord. Make a straight path to repentance. In all the ways you have deserted the way of God, turn back to it now. In any way you have devalued or emptied yourself of the presence of Jesus Christ, I implore you to be forgiven and receive power to live a holy, upstanding, noble, and peace-filled life.

The Beginning of Sorrows

Jesus warns us the first sign of his coming is the prevailing tendency for deceit to be our customary speech. We have so many lies and opinions of men parading as facts and truth; trust in what is shared over our public airwaves is at an all-time low. As detailed by Mike Flynn on September 21, 2012 in Breitbart.com, Gallup shares that "60% of Americans, an all-time high, do not trust the mass media to accurately or fairly report the news. Mind you, that isn't 60% of Republicans or conservatives, but Americans of all political persuasions." No wonder there is confusion and apathy towards our media.

Even if you search for the truth, you cannot find it. With the internet we can find almost anything, right? Yes, but not necessarily the truth. The internet does not rank things according to truth so we are free to keep on looking until we find information that says what we want to hear. What reinforces our way is deemed reliable and what doesn't reaffirm our own biases and confirm our prejudices is deemed suspect. If we are not careful we will continually shrink our thinking and make ourselves a person of smaller and smaller concerns. Our life will move away from the epic story of grace God is narrating through us to become another episode of reality TV or shuffling through a series of levels in this game we call life.

These are the days for important things to happen. These are days of repentance. These are the days for aligning yourself with Jesus Christ. What will be the indicators God is calling you to the truth of his good news? The first will be the liars. How do you know people are lying? They have their mouth open.

When I was growing up we were not allowed to use the word "lie" or "liars". People told the truth or told "stories". Lying was meant to be such a rare thing our parents didn't even want us to use the word. Now, lying is more common than dirt. When I was young, your word was your bond, your guarantee. Now, it is a means of escape that allows for plausible deniability if and when things go badly.

Jesus said, "Watch out that no one deceives you, for many will come in my name, claiming, 'I am the Christ', and will deceive many." (Matthew 24: 4 -5) In other words, many will say that Jesus is their reference point; the foundation of their actions is based on Jesus. But, you can't believe it. You have to verify it. Jesus said in Matthew chapter seven there is narrow way of doing this. Observe the fruit or results of what people do. And ask the question, does the way they produce these results rise from their adherence to the golden rule? These are our standards for living free of deception.

Many will claim they are the anointed one for this time and this season we all face. John Stossel in his book, *No, They Can't,* warns us of this: "What intuition tempts us to believe: the important thing is to have heroic leaders. What reality taught me: Real leaders don't control other people's lives." Do not be deceived. Jesus compels by grace through faith for us to follow. The deceivers will compel by government force, through the intimidation of the media mob majority, or by any means of coercion possible.

The Apostle Paul in Romans 2: 4 urges us to understand that it is easy for us to misunderstand the reality of things, "not realizing that God's kindness leads you toward repentance". This is the first and tell-tale sign for us to have on our radar screen when it comes to the agendas and gospels of the deceivers. A deceiver will give us an easy way out and tell us let's keep on sinning that grace may abound. You will not be expected to change and sacrifice without requiring of others who are more fortunate than you to act first.

But there will be no delay or postponement given us by the truth. The first thing any truth-filled message will do will be to ready us for God's judgment of our predicament, turn us back in repentance, and align us to God's ways in as direct a way as possible. So, "watch out", Jesus says and don't be deceived.

The second indicator we are moving towards the second coming of Jesus is "you will hear of wars and rumors of wars, but see to it that you are not alarmed. Such things must happen, but the end is still to come." (Matthew 24: 6) It's easy to carry no sense of alarm if we remain ignorant of what is going on in the world. A Saturday morning at my house looks and feels very peaceful. I wake up to the "Please" of my granddaughter asking nicely for someone to get her out of the bed. The most dramatic occurrence is changing a dirty diaper. We have breakfast. I carry the trash off and things seem very tranquil. Someone is having a yard sale along the side of the road. The sun is shining. Is there anything that calls for our repentance?

Yes, on the day I write this paragraph, in countries in Europe and in South America there is a run on the banks. Russia was testing ballistic missiles this week. There was another massacre reported in Syria. An Iranian general says their finger is on the "war trigger". Another fatal shooting occurred overnight. The rumors abound: militaristic and economic consumption is either encouraged and pushed or is called to be cut off or put under the strictest of restraints. Even in the trying-to-be-pleasant world of our homes, the despair over lowered expectations or lack of peace wages war on our psyche.

This brings us to the third sign calling us to repentance: "nation will rise against nation". I can't help but think of the United States and China. Some would say it is merely what goes around comes around. We are trillions of dollars in debt to China yet we send them foreign aid. One nation's rise is built upon the other. All of Europe is trying to hold together. Will Germany rise upon the outcome of Greece or Spain or Portugal or France? All could fall like dominoes if one defaults. We have not looked to the Lord but have bound ourselves together in what Glen Beck calls "mutually assured economic destruction."

What of "kingdom against kingdom"? Everywhere division and factions abound. Some call for compromise but the division of sin has moved us to become unable to bend our way back to the common ground of repentance. We cannot admit to our ongoing suspicions and our own bias. We have justified ourselves and told the present generations our problem is not that we have betrayed the Lord and chosen the wrong way as an explanation for things going wrong. No, the reason we feel like we're headed in the wrong direction is because we do not have unanimous consent. Only if the naysayers are removed or silenced, do we have any hopes of having the right side (our side) prevail. We are unable to hear the words of Jeremiah the prophet, "My people have committed two sins: They have forsaken me, the spring of living water, and have dug their own cisterns, broken cisterns that cannot hold water." (Jeremiah 2: 13)

Why should we repent? Consider how dry we are to the word of God? Consider how man made rules keep wells of water from irrigating the land for food production? People lament the limited resources we have yet we do not move in faith in response to God's word. "When I shut up the heavens so that there is no rain, or command locusts to devour the land or send a plague among my people, if my people, who are called by my name, will humble themselves and pray and seek my face and turn from their wicked ways, then will I hear from heaven and will forgive their sin and will heal their land." (2 Chronicles 7: 13 – 14)

A decade ago we experienced drought here in Virginia. We were moving to ration the water in the Roanoke Valley. The water level in the reservoir was said to be nearing the point of being unable to be replenished without it taking years. The short version of the story was: we prayed, the Lord sent rain in the remnants of a hurricane and the reservoir was filled to overflowing within two weeks. I had seen a similar answer come when we prayed for rain in Kentucky.

But, the scripture highlights here the extreme measures God will allow in his goodness to turn us to repentance, including plaques of drought, fire, famine, pests, and pestilence. Most arise out of man's inhumanity to man, sinners sinning against each other. Strange diseases and even stranger maladies affecting people should drive us to ask the awesome God to reveal his grace in awesome ways.

Finally, the scripture warns us we are called to repentance through "earthquakes in various places". Yes, we are going to be shaken, as the dream foretold and in countless other ways. Already, Japan has experienced its shaking with the accompanying tsunami and destruction. Our nation's "big one" is on the horizon.

Think back to the words of my dream, "I'll deal with you in another way." I thought of these words as I followed the progress of Hurricane Sandy. The largest storm in our modern recording of storms with tropical storm winds felt over 800 miles from the center of the storm. Record low barometric pressure readings fell as the confluence of weather conditions created the perfect, catastrophic storm.

But, this storm and others have brought forth no national repentance. The media has kept silent over the ongoing devastation and grief felt by those in New York and elsewhere. We have to remind ourselves, these are the beginning of sorrows. These are the warning signs that call us to repentance.

A Question of Faith

Jesus says, when the last days unfold before he comes again, there will be hostility against his name. We expect this hostility from those who follow false religions or those who say they have no religion yet who are irritated by grace and truth. What alarms us in our day are the attacks by those in authority in our own nation labeling Christians as extremists and threats to the nation's security. Long gone are the days of statesman and orator Daniel Webster who said, "No government can be secure which is not supported by moral habits... whatever makes men good Christians, makes them good citizens." (December 22, 1820, Bicentennial Celebration of the Landing at Plymouth Rock, Massachusetts)

Persecution can prove to be a good thing. It defines and refines those who truly belong and believe. But, woe, to any nation that persecutes God's people. Woe to any nation that elevates sin and normalizes rude or vulgar behavior.

Persecution comes in many forms. It is revealed in attacks on orthodoxy and faith-driven practices and in physical attacks against the faithful. Persecution can come from promoting a distorted or false image of what a Christian is. Persecution can come when people face a double standard of harassment or the limiting of their rights because of their beliefs. It may arise because of inaction or the ignoring of consequences when we are unwilling to defend the rights and freedoms we have. We have witnessed all of these in our nation, ranging from the Internal Revenue Service's targeting of groups, to the Justice Department's wholesale seizing of Associated Press records, to the judge in Michigan suppressing the freedom of speech and assembly to Christians because those hearing their message threatened violence against them. Unfortunately persecution can rise from within the Christian community as proselytizing and evangelism are frowned upon and discouraged and where those who "contend for the faith that was once for all entrusted to God's holy people" (Jude 1: 3) are branded as anti-intellectuals, close minded, unloving and prejudiced in their ignorance.

Persecution is a working out of the principle that accompanies consolidation. It is the work of sifting out who doesn't fit or belong. Back when I grew up my grandmother would make bread in the pantry just off the kitchen in her house. She would first gather the flour out of the flour bin and then she would sift it out onto the counter. Both good and evil will follow this process in the last days. Each faction will try to gather as many constituents as possible. Then they will push for solidarity and loyalty. Those who will not join the evil crowd of the committed will be demonized, ostracized, and assaulted.

Those who do not follow the way of Jesus will be lost and miss out on the joy, peace, and righteousness of the kingdom. Will you be forced into a theocracy to save you? No! No Christian will force that upon you. There is no Christian version of sharia.

Do we want to legislate to a standard that has a high, universal, moral code? Yes, of course we do, but we want that standard to recognize the law is meant to punish the wicked not restrict or condemn the noble. Laws, in order for them to be more than just the rules of despotic men, must apply to all, equally, no matter the time or place or person.

Our hope as a Christian, our hope as a nation is for us to have an unavoidable experience of God's grace in our lives. We believe the Judeo-Christian principles of life, liberty, and the rights of an individual to his or her own property are the foundation stones upon which a society and an economy are best built. We know that God is at work to consummate and complete all of his redemptive acts in Jesus Christ. God is unchanging. God is at work. The question is what part of his work will be our responsibility? When God moves in power will we see it as an act of redemption or an act of retribution? What will be your perspective? What will you believe? Can suffering, death, and persecution serve a higher purpose? Will animus and hatred mark you as an enemy or a friend of God?

Can you face death as Jesus did? How did Jesus die? He died forgiving those who killed him. He died knowing he was at work along with the Father. He died having seen to the care of his mother. He died expecting to see someone join him in paradise. He died content with entrusting his life to the Father. If something has to give, can you? Can you be content if you lose everything, or will you lose it in the days ahead?

Can you face death? You can if you can face Jesus now. Receive his love for you. No matter what you have done or what has been done to you Jesus can fill the void and heal the aching. Jesus can lift every burden you carry. Jesus has already satisfied the justice for which you crave.

The Scandal of Being Offended

"I am not ashamed of the gospel", the Apostle Paul confessed. I join him in that confession from Romans 1: 16. But, many so-called Christians today do seem to be ashamed. "A few years ago, the annual national Episcopal convention overwhelmingly refused even to consider a resolution affirming that Jesus Christ is Lord". (http://www.theblaze.com/stories/cross-dressing-clergy-these-are-the-reasons-the-episcopal-church-could-be-near-collapse/)

Throughout the church there is a kudzu-like creeping of heresies and self-assertions that seek to dismiss the atoning work of Jesus, both in its power to redeem from sin or to judge sin in its conception or its fuller consequences.

Being masters of our own fate has become more spiritual than trusting in an 'absentee misogynist, racist, homophobic, patronizing, despotic, mythical creature'. Of course, these mischaracterizations of our Heavenly Father can only be put forth when we reject the clear teachings of Jesus and turn against the work of the Holy Spirit.

The rush to say all ways have validity or credibility in getting people to heaven or into eternal life contradict Jesus on several fronts. The gospels are full of references to the exclusive and unique authority Jesus holds to forgive sins, command nature, cast out the demonic, heal the sick, raise the dead, and to preach good news to the poor. Never mind, the revelation of John 14: 6 where Jesus says, "I am the way and the truth and the life. No one comes to the Father except through me." The progressives maintain they can make progress to God despite Jesus' words to the contrary.

But, let me illustrate why Jesus is the only way and why that is a good thing. Have you ever ordered furniture and had it shipped to you? The box arrived and there on the outside of the box was the picture of the desk you imagined was perfect for your home office. You rushed to open the box, pull out the pieces, and put them together. The instructions and a listing of all the necessary pieces were there inside and step by step you followed those instructions until "Tada!" There before you, was the beautiful desk you ordered.

But, what if you had opened the box and pulled out the pieces and the instructions and pieces inside were for a bookshelf. You quickly check the front of your box against what you see in front of you on the floor and you immediately call the company from which you ordered the furniture. They've got to make things right.

Imagine your surprise when they tell you all furniture pieces lead to the furniture you want. You do not believe that for a second and you would never do business with a company that is foolish enough to assert that.

You demand they send you what you ordered, not just a box with the correct picture outside but the parts and instructions inside to match.

That sense of outrage and righteous indignation should be applied in the same way to yourself if you try to pass off the all-roads-lead-to-heaven myth. The pieces and parts for life presented by Buddha or Mohammed cannot and will not bring you into conformity with Jesus. Following Jesus and his call and prognosis for your life is the sole means of making progress to God. Other religions are not generic equivalents. They are more akin to placebos that work by faith but leave us dead to the realities of grace.

False Prophets

There are three tests you can give to the prophet to see if they are false or true. The first is the temptation test. The second is the confirmation test. The third is the salvation test. Put simply, a true prophet will not be interested in his version of the story but will insist on "Thus saith the Lord." This is not cop out or camouflage but a transparency about the message. The prophet is not omniscient or authoritative in themselves. If their message is messed up, they assume responsibility. The prophet doesn't presume he has a message from God. He instead as the Apostle Paul stated desires to embrace willingly the obligation to preach the good news. (I Corinthians 9: 16)

My dream is good news and prophetic in that it is an impulse towards repentance. Its revelation and the call it places on our life as a nation is to "lead us not into temptation." I may not be a prophet. I don't claim to be. I just feel obligated to set the dream forth and you can decide where it will lead you. If God has anything to do with it, I know one thing: it will lead you to repentance and a reevaluation of your relationship with God.

It will challenge you to remove the redundancies of sin in your life and to clarify the calling God has placed on your life.

The false prophet will call you to a new life of faith and strength, of blessing and life without repentance. You will be told you can discover this for yourself. If a higher power is necessary by all means take advantage of what the Universe offers; go for it.

The first temptation of the false prophet is to get you to question the goodness of God. They won't be forced into a lie if they can get you to provide lies for yourself, to scripturally put yourself in a position of not being able to see the spiritual forest for the trees. The false prophet will not ask you to compare scripture to scripture to expose ancient foundations of truth. The false prophet will ask you to compare scripture with our modern understanding or to our postmodern thinking. The temptation is to move from the priority of obedience to God being steadfast to our openness to God being steadfast.

In the book *Moving at the Speed of Grace* I share three great temptations. The first is 'love me and leave me alone'. God, let me live my life the way I choose and welcome me home when I am done. If I am free and if you love me you will let me live my life without judging it. Thus the first temptation questions the goodness of God and asks us to forget that God is faithful and just. The first temptation is to require God to still be faithful when we have spent our lifetime running after something else.

The second temptation is to 'jump track' trying to get credit for a life of grace while still being rooted to sin. This temptation is to travel the moral high ground of our own opinion, to seek strength in our stubbornness, and to help those who will appreciate what we have to offer. We are good people who do good things so a good God is bound to take us in when all is said and done.

The third temptation is to shortcut the way of grace, picking and choosing our way according to our own self-interest and comfort. But how do you take a shortcut down a straight and narrow path? You try to skip what you don't know or like to get to what you do. We move towards faith without repentance. What happens? Jesus said the word of grace gets stolen as quickly as it is sown that way. Our faith fades in light of difficulty, scrutiny, or persecution or our faith gets crowded out and choked by other concerns.

The second test we must administer in this time of false prophets is the confirmation test. This involves two things: congruence with God's word and name and actual confirmation or congruence between what the prophet says and what comes to pass. The first congruence is more important than the second. Let the prophet Isaiah speak to this. "Consult God's instruction and the testimony of warning. If anyone does not speak according to this word, they have no light of dawn." (Isaiah 8: 20)

This is especially important to remember in these days where arguments are won not because they reflect the truth of God's word but because they result in satisfying our senses.

The third test is the salvation test. Does the scenario described and prescribed by the prophet bring you to God? Again Isaiah says, "The LORD Almighty is the one you are to regard as holy, he is the one you are to fear, he is the one you are to dread." (Isaiah 8: 13) If the motivator's words do not move you towards Jesus Christ then move away from that person. Better yet, go back to the prophets of the Bible and read them. See what they say. The true prophet first and foremost focuses your attention away from himself, even while he may be a billboard for God's message like Hosea naming his children to reflect the judgment upon the nation. Yet, as judgment is declared so is the result of turning around to trust in God.

The prophet Jonah, reluctantly preached, "Yet forty days, and Nineveh shall be overthrown," (Jonah 3: 4) but his reluctance was because he knew God's call to repent is meant to save. Jonah prayed after seeing Nineveh turn from their wickedness and violence, "Isn't this what I said, LORD, when I was still at home? That is what I tried to forestall by fleeing to Tarshish. I knew that you are a gracious and compassionate God, slow to anger and abounding in love, a God who relents from sending calamity." (Jonah 4: 2)

I pray the judgment revealed in my dream can be forestalled and postponed indefinitely.   Unlike Jonah and Nineveh, I do not want the United States to be overthrown. I pray for our leaders to emulate the actions of Nineveh's leader who stepped down from his throne, took off his mantle of power, and humbled himself in repentance, not only setting an example but proclaiming a fast of repentance and prayer to every inhabitant and creature in Nineveh.

This kind of action is what I had hoped for in 2008 when the Emergency Economic Stabilization Act was pushed through the congress. How much different would our situation be today if President Bush had humbled himself and called on Americans to support one another rather than expect some outside stimulus package to solve our problems without changing our ways. Instead, the President reached for a solution against his principles. "I've abandoned free market principles to save the free market system." Was it really saved or did we just postpone the day of reckoning? Would we have needed the waste of trillions of dollars if the nine Americans who were doing okay had been asked to band together to help the one neighbor that wasn't?

The call to humility and charity still waits to be sounded. Meanwhile, the false prophets live lavishly as they preach a salvation of sacrifice and restraint. They put shackles on the law abiding while saying they are stopping the law breakers. They will take their own temperature and pronounce the nation recovered. If anyone has doubts, they have assured the rest of us they will extract from the one what the ninety-nine need to continue to live without repentance. Somehow, I feel no assurance of safety.

An Increase in Wickedness

It doesn't take a rocket scientist or even an astute observer of the times to notice that we have lost our moorings to the moral and spiritual foundations with which we began as a nation. I suppose as we get older we grow nostalgic about the way things used to be but even an old man knows you can go faster downhill than climbing back up.

Jesus here warns (let's translate Matthew 24: 12 literally for a moment) 'because lawlessness increases, many go psycho.' The breath and energy to be upright is knocked right out of people. Then, when the losses pile up, they lose it. We pin our hopes on the promises and the persona of our leaders and we are bound to be disappointed.

What does it mean to be lawless? What does it mean for lawlessness to multiply or increase? I think we know what it is to go psycho or as the King James puts it, for "the love of many shall wax cold". But, what's the fallout? And what are the antidotes for our nation to be healed from this piercing?

To be lawless has nothing to do with how many laws you have. We are inundated with rules, regulations, mandates, and laws. Our tax code alone runs 73,608 pages and being edited upward as you read. The Affordable Health Care Act (Obamacare) with its accompanying citations ran about 2700 pages when it was passed. Since then, over 13,000 pages have been written to get ready for implementation. Some experts estimate we add 80,000 pages of regulations each year. So, lawlessness can arise from the overwhelming number of laws as well as from too few.

The Merriam-Webster Dictionary defines lawlessness as "not constrained or controlled by law." The time of the judges in the Bible reflects this attitude: "In those days there was no king in Israel; every man did that which was right in their own eyes." (Judges 17: 6, 21: 25 KJV) This is the way of a fool because a fool won't listen to wise counsel. (Proverbs 12: 15) Have we become a nation of fools?

What are the common signs of lawlessness we need to address? The first is the degradation of our language. Oh, how we need to clean up the coarseness of our speech, cut out the cussing, and choose vocabulary that gets our point across without 'talking ugly'. Political correctness is another form of degradation. You can't speak of someone who breaks the law as an illegal. You cannot call one who follows jihad a jihadist. The deconstruction of definitions and meaning to suit whatever cause de jour we are pursuing is another way of degradation. The whole homosexual marriage debate is based on the degradation of the plain spoken definition of marriage Jesus gives in the gospel of Mark. Jesus declares the construction of marriage is derived from the created order where God "at the beginning of creation God 'made them male and female'... Therefore what God has joined together, let no one separate." (Mark 10: 6, 9) Statistical lying is another form of degradation. Unemployment decreases while the number of unemployed goes up. How does that jive together? Statistical lying is reporting to suit an agenda rather than the facts.

Another sign of lawlessness is the destruction or diminishing of standards. This can be done by removing any logical consistency to our thinking as well as the well-intentioned but destructive idealism many have. *My way has to work because it is my way. My good intentions insure a good outcome.* This reminds us of another proverb: "**There is a way that appears to be right, but in the end it leads to death.**" (Proverbs 14: 12, 16: 25) This death could be the end of a conversation, the end of discovering options for moving forward, or the end of civilization as we know it.

I remember one outbreak of this spirit of lawlessness back in August of 2008. I was having a conversation with a nice young lady in the bookstore. We had agreed on what would be appropriate steps to take for every issue we had discussed until she asked me, "Are you planning to vote for Senator Obama?" I told her I could not but before I had a chance to enumerate my reasons she stuck up her hand and said, "We'll just have to agree to disagree." I asked, "About what?"

Up until that time we had no disagreements. My unwillingness to vote for now President Obama cut off all conversation. She was unwilling to explain why she was going to vote for him. There was no need for explanation. I couldn't even talk to the hand, because she was walking away from me.

When this happens the lawless will provide no explanation for why things are being used against us. We will be presumed guilty. The lawless carries no responsibility for the problems he or she creates or uncovers. All of this is someone else's fault. The problem with this kind of lawlessness is the problem of all blame. You cannot fix that which is another person's responsibility. It's like trying to play doubles in tennis and only one person is reaching to return the ball.

Another side of this same problem is the selective enforcement or non-enforcement of standards. The goal is to turn all of us into lawbreakers. Selective enforcement provides leverage to control us and bring us into bondage. Non-enforcement produces injustice, despair, and anarchy. If problems cannot or will not be tackled by appropriate authorities then people feel justified into taking matters into their own hands. Distrust supersedes the due diligence established by law and that lack of faith is a dissolving agent to civil society.

The third way lawlessness is expressed is in the devaluing of life. This occurs because of greed and contempt. Human trafficking, printing money for votes, slave labor, prostitution, acting as a mule for drugs are all signs of our lack of care for each other. Minds are desensitized by violence. Love and life has been administered by prescription or outsourced to TV and gaming. The education of our children, their development, has been turned over to a bureaucracy of people who train our children to be minions of the state. One news anchor calmly chastises us for thinking our own children are our responsibility. "We have to break through our kind of private idea that kids belong to their parents or kids belong to their families and recognize that kids belong to whole communities." (MSNBC anchor, Melissa Harris-Perry)

Yes, I know from personal experience the government does not always have *the best interest of the child* in mind. Yes, I have seen for myself as abuse was covered up, negligence and incompetence defended; theft and lies rationalized, and children returned to dysfunctional and dangerous settings. No one is immune from this corruption. But, our calling from God is to add value to life not take it away.

One more example of the lawlessness that devalues life has to be mentioned: abortion. Abortion is the fruit of a godless societal tree. And, what society can endure that is for the choice to kill its children before they can experience life for themselves? What nation should endure when government funds are provided for its extermination?

How bad is it? Here is an excerpt from an article by Marc Thiessen published April 8, 2013.

"Testifying against a Florida bill that would require abortionists to provide emergency medical care to an infant who survives an abortion, Planned Parenthood lobbyist Alisa LaPolt Snow was asked point blank: "If a baby is born on a table as a result of a botched abortion, what would Planned Parenthood want to have happen to that child that is struggling for life?" She replied: "We believe that any decision that's made should be left up to the woman, her family, and the physician. Jaws in the committee room dropped. Asked again, she repeated her answer.

Only after a firestorm erupted in the conservative media did Planned Parenthood issue a statement that in the "extremely unlikely and highly unusual" event that a baby were born alive it would "provide appropriate care to both the woman and the infant." That is debatable, since a Planned Parenthood counselor has been caught on tape admitting that the organization leaves infants born alive after an abortion to die. But if Planned Parenthood really does provide such care, why was it lobbying against a bill requiring such care in the first place?

The fact is, it is not as unusual for children to be left to die after a failed abortion as some might think. Right now in Philadelphia, abortionist Kermit Gosnell is on trial for the murder of seven infants who were born alive. According to District Attorney Seth Williams, Gosnell "induced labor, forced the live birth of viable babies in the sixth, seventh, eighth month of pregnancy and then killed those babies by cutting into the back of the neck with scissors and severing their spinal cord." Prosecutors said that Gosnell ended hundreds of pregnancies in this way. "These killings became so routine that no one could put an exact number on them. They were considered 'standard procedure.' "

Abortion is the tap root of our nation's suicide. It is the instrument of black genocide in the United States. It is the vehicle that utopian planners drive toward their great society. The call is upon us to repent, to retain our horror over the death of innocents and not give in to the convenience of medically assisted choices. Our call is to choose life, to provide loving environments and examples from which others benefit. Our call is to adopt a different way.

Without repentance, we will all soon be judged for our use and benefit to society. Will our quality of life warrant us continuance or will our life come to an abrupt and aborted end?

What Will Be Your Testimony?

Christ does not hide from us nor are his ways shrouded beyond our understanding. On the contrary, they are plain in their humility, self-evident in their truth, self-explanatory in their love and discipline. The question is will the difference Jesus makes be the difference in you and how you conduct yourself?

Jesus' last warning urges us to remember "the one who stands firm to the end will be saved. And this gospel of the kingdom will be preached in the whole world as a testimony to all nations, and then the end will come." (Matthew 24: 13 – 14) Jesus' coming again will not be a clandestine movement. "For as lightning that comes from the east is visible even in the west, so will the coming of the Son of Man be." (Matthew 24: 27)

But, what will be our testimony? It does not take privilege or secret knowledge or any particular quality or genius to uncover the grace of Jesus Christ. Jesus said it is as simple as expressing your thirst. "Let anyone who is thirsty come to me and drink. Whoever believes in me, as Scripture has said, rivers of living water will flow from within them." (John 7: 37 – 38) Admit your weariness. "Come to me, all you who are weary and burdened, and I will give you rest." (Matthew 11: 28) Cry out for a full and substantial life. "The thief comes only to steal and kill and destroy; I have come that they may have life, and have it to the full. I am the good shepherd. The good shepherd lays down his life for the sheep." (John 10: 10 – 11)

Jesus has been pierced for us. Why would we any longer want to be a nation pierced?

Group Questions

1. Is it easier for you to see the work of God operating on a grand scale today or does the presence of evil dominate the way you see things? In what ways are you preparing for the second coming of Jesus Christ?

2. How do you share your joy in Jesus Christ? How do you avoid the temptation of being offended by the gospel? How do you share the exclusive claim of Jesus to be "the way, the truth, and the life"?

3. What makes a prophet a false one? Who in our day offers solutions without repentance? How do you guard against false prophets? Can you compare and contrast what the scripture says with what the media or what personalities in the media say?

4. What are the ways you have witnessed the spirit of lawlessness? What areas of your life have you despaired of changing, even thought of going psycho a time or two? How are you standing with Jesus to overcome this lawlessness and renew the strength of your love and hope?

5. What is your testimony concerning Jesus? Do you know the sound of his voice? Have you received the life of his Spirit? Do you move forward in the strength of his forgiveness? How have you found rest for your soul in Him? How has Jesus satisfied your thirst for life?

The Days of Noah

The LORD saw how great the wickedness of the human race had become on the earth, and that every inclination of the thoughts of the human heart was only evil all the time... But Noah found favor in the eyes of the LORD." (Genesis 6: 5, 8)

Yes, what will be our testimony? Will we be caught repeating the days of Noah, "eating and drinking, marrying and giving in marriage, up to the day Noah entered the ark"? (Matthew 24: 38) It has been fourteen years since my dream occurred. Who is to say when and if it will be fulfilled? When it doesn't happen one year it is easy to say (or pray) it won't happen the next year. Noah preached for one hundred twenty years warning those of his generation that a flood was coming.

One way to view this time frame is to know with each passing year we are drawing closer to judgment being fulfilled. The normal way to think is Noah is a crazy fool wasting his breath and his energy building an ark in a place where no ark is needed. The normal way to think is if judgment hadn't come by now it's not coming at all.

The Normalcy Bias

This normalcy bias is standard not only for Noah's day but holds true for every generation since the Fall. Things will continue on as they have always been. "It was the same in the days of Lot. People were eating and drinking, buying and selling, planting and building. But the day Lot left Sodom, fire and sulfur rained down from heaven and destroyed them all.

It will be just like this on the day the Son of Man is revealed." (Luke 17: 28-30)

Jesus said we can go about our normal routine but that is no deterrent to him breaking through and being revealed in our day. What is normal anyway? Is it normal to speculate? Should I fly to Las Vegas and lay a bet down on an earthquake occurring on 6/22? Are you talking to your bookie? It's normal for most of us to act in haste or fear. Don't believe me? Go to the grocery store ahead of a storm and watch how people act.

What is normal is to brace ourselves for impact in a crash but what if you don't know when the crash will occur? After a while you just go about your business.

That works if you choose ahead of time what you will do in the case of a real emergency. You rehearse. You keep supplies on hand and you hope for the best. You could be like my friend the Rev. Bill Johnson who when I shared my dream and suggested he might want to be outside of California on June 22 said, "Norm, God has called me to be here. If the earthquake happens and I survive, I will be ready to help." And, I know he will.

We all have a bias for what is our normal. In light of Jesus' words we want to make sure our normal includes more than eating and drinking, marrying and giving in marriage. We want to make sure our normal has forsaken operating out of bitterness compounding our unbelief with despair when the reality that hit the fan gets blown our way. We want to make sure our normal follows the way of grace and compounds our faith in the power of God's strength and promise.

Let what is normal for you change so you are on the ark when the flood comes. Let what is normal for you be "God is our refuge and strength, an ever-present help in trouble. Therefore we will not fear, though the earth gives way and the mountains fall into the heart of the sea, though its waters roar and foam and the mountains quake with their surging." (Psalm 46: 1 – 3)

A Resistance to the Truth

How do I know this was a problem that marked the days of Noah? I read these words. "I am going to bring floodwaters on the earth to destroy all life under the heavens, every creature that has the breath of life in it. Everything on earth will perish. But I will establish my covenant with you, and you will enter the ark." (Genesis 6: 17 – 18a) The entrance requirements for the ark were based on entry into covenant with God. It was a free standing offer. We can each be like Noah and find "favor in the eyes of the Lord". (Genesis 6: 8)

But, you can't find it if you are apathetic in seeking God's favor or if you turn your back to the Lord. The proof is in the pudding. Eight souls were saved through the flood. Everyone else closed the door of their mind and heart before the door of the ark was closed on them.

Does this describe your relationship with God and the things of God? Are you seeking Him with all of your heart or have you moved on to more interesting things? Have you put God's word on hold while you carry on other conversations? You got the call; you just haven't returned it, yet.

Have you ever tried to call someone and all circuits were busy? You get cut off when you most wanted to have an opportunity to speak. This is your life without truth. There's so much static and interference when connected you can't hear and your words are wasted breath.

Truth endures because it is unshakable. It is not eroded by popular opinion. It can always be heard through the static and the noise. It is the light that shines in the darkness and in the rubble of judgment it is a beacon to shelter and safety. Don't resist it. Take in as much as you can. Use every resource to acquire it. Get to know it. Wrap yourself up in it.

God says through the prophet Jeremiah, "Go up and down the streets of Jerusalem, look around and consider, search through her squares. If you can find but one person who deals honestly and seeks the truth, I will forgive this city." (Jeremiah 5: 1) Don't resist the truth. Your embrace of the truth can save a city.

The Prevalence of Wickedness

"The LORD saw how great the wickedness of the human race had become on the earth, and that every inclination of the thoughts of the human heart was only evil all the time." (Genesis 6: 5) Can you see it?

We have violence in our nation. We have our perpetrators. We have our braggarts and our bullies. We have those who condone it and those who excuse it. We have those who follow it and broadcast it. We have the gawkers and squawkers, our flash mobs and stalkers. We have those who are paranoid because of violence. We have those who must defend us against the violence. There are protectors and rejecters, policemen and pacifists. There are those who are thoughtful reflectors. They study the violence, speak and lecture about it, write and publish about it. We have those who reflect on its roots and its reasons and elaborate often on all its malfeasance. We have creators and gamers, gangbangers, gainsayers. There is not a single day or single moment that goes by when it doesn't continually incline its influence upon our thoughts. "Just as it was in the days of Noah, so also will it be in the days of the Son of Man." (Luke 17: 26)

When I was a young boy, I would tell you I witnessed very little violence. Wild animals and a few wild people occasionally interrupted our day to day routine. Assassinations and war were part of the evening news but I paid more attention to the heroic adventures of my mind. My brother and I had our conflicts, our dirt clod fights, our rough and tumble moments but that's all they were – moments. I hypothesized that violence was part of life, a natural result of the Fall. Accidents happen. We can be hurt. People can be mean.

Of course when I went off to college I learned that violence was not the problem of a sinner's disposition. Violence didn't lash out from a heart gone bad. Violence had become institutionalized. It occupied a leadership position in the hallways and backrooms of power. It arose from the multiple webs of bureaucracy that were spinning out of control. It was rapidly expanding through the military industrial complex. The violence of a single individual we could always attribute to these systemic or environmental conditions. Besides, Jesus forgave the individual sinner. It was the person who had a position and an office, the wielders of power and influence who were the greedy SOBs we had to fix.

God was dead. Jesus was mighty to save the individual but these human systems were beyond his power but thankfully not ours.

Thankfully, we now have begun to place better people within these structures and systems who will work violence out of our institutions like so much detritus being flushed away, right? "We are the change we have been waiting for", right? Thankfully, all of those who railed against the *man* in their youth are now the man we were waiting for someone to be and we need not fear what these men or women might do, right?

Wrong!

The call for a solution to violence remains unchanged. Something has to give. Thankfully, "God so loved the world that he gave his one and only Son, that whoever believes in him shall not perish but have eternal life. For God did not send his Son into the world to condemn the world, but to save the world through him... This is the verdict: Light has come into the world, but people loved darkness instead of light because their deeds were evil. Everyone who does evil hates the light, and will not come into the light for fear that their deeds will be exposed. But whoever lives by the truth comes into the light, so that it may be seen plainly that what they have done has been done in the sight of God." (John 3: 16 – 17, 19 - 21)

Inclination towards Heroes or Giants in the Land (The Return of the Nephilim)

Our celebrity culture, our elevation of being famous over being faithful, our desire for recognition over righteousness will all bring forth judgment. God's first commands out of his top ten says, "You shall have no other gods before me. You shall not make for yourself an image in the form of anything in heaven above or on the earth beneath or in the waters below. You shall not bow down to them or worship them; for I, the LORD your God, am a jealous God, punishing the children for the sin of the parents to the third and fourth generation of those who hate me, but showing love to a thousand generations of those who love me and keep my commandments." (Exodus 20: 3 – 6)

Soon, technology and all we do will bring us to a point of singularity and advancement. Some believe we won't miss the mark anymore. We will adapt and evolve beyond what we have ever been. Good people will take care of bad people. Of course we do not question the possibility of the good people becoming the bad people. That's already been ruled out so that won't happen. The future is bright. We are definitely on the road to recovery and greater success.

Some are longing for the day when they will be more than human. Literature, the arts, and entertainment all glorify the immortals, the demi-gods, and those who will stand as our avengers against the greater powers arrayed to deny us our full potential. Transhumanists and others seek to genetically and technologically engineer a new face to the age-old demonic claim, "your eyes will be opened, and you will be like God". (Genesis 3: 5) Meanwhile, I'm sure the "sons of God" wouldn't mind another run with "the daughters of men". Let's discontinue our search for heroes and quit defying the One True God. Go ahead and watch the movie: Iron Man 3, Superman, Wolverine, Percy Jackson, et cetera; just remember it's only a movie.

I hope we can navigate a straight and narrow way between avoiding idolizing the designated or demonic hero of the day while appreciating the advances and opportunities of technology. We will soon find out if we can.

One last word of warning about our inclination towards needing a hero; the scripture teaches the rise of the Anti-Christ will be built on top of that desire. This is why I pray we will have this affirmation settled in our mind and heart. "May I never boast except in the cross of our Lord Jesus Christ, through which the world has been crucified to me, and I to the world. Neither circumcision nor uncircumcision means anything; what counts is the new creation. Peace and mercy to all who follow this rule." (Galatians 6: 14 – 16a)

Eyes on Jesus, everybody!

Denial of God's Judgment

Many desire what God ultimately promises! Immortality, greater wisdom, a glorified body, an abundance of peace and joy, But, they don't want to wait for it or have to die to get to it. Many have no faith or assurance the promise's fulfillment will be forthcoming but God always keeps his promises. God always sustains his truth!

How can America consider itself to be immune from God's judgment? If God's chosen people were not spared how can we continue on our path without it coming to a dead end?

Have you ever seen a forest fire? Ever watched a thousand acres burn? It doesn't happen all at once. The fire smolders at times. Sometimes it is pushed by the wind; it races and explodes in its own heat. Sometimes it marches forward, fueled by whatever lies in its path. In the days of Noah, the fire burned for a hundred and twenty years and then it was snuffed out as the rains began and the door of the ark was closed.

For a hundred and twenty years life raged upon the earth. The demonic sons of God sought out their pleasure and the goals of their genetic manipulation through the daughters of men. Creatures of myth and legend, giants among men, *nephilim* ruled and corrupted generations of people. Noah alone was found untainted by the wickedness of his culture and age. His faith and influence saved his family, marked him as a man obedient to God, and condemned the world in which he lived.

I cannot imagine the ridicule, the threats, the isolation Noah must have experienced for those years of preparation. Yet, God spoke and gave him instructions. God gave him a task to fulfill. Noah "found grace in the eyes of the Lord." (Genesis 6: 8 KJV) The distinguishing judgment upon Noah's life, the experience that spoke of Noah living up to his name was that the favor of God could come and rest upon him.

Imagine being asked by a friend to come into their home to see the new tablecloth they purchased. You walk in and there before you is the most lavish and exquisite piece of material you have ever seen. The intricacy and depth of design captures your mind and you stand stunned trying to capture words to express how unbelievably beautiful it is. Then, your mouth drops as your friend tells you how much he spent to get it.

You step over to make a closer inspection and your friend warns you not to rest your hand too heavily upon it. You draw back not wanting to offend your friend when he adds, "The table won't bear your weight."

What? The table? Curious, you reach over and pull the corner of the tablecloth up only to see the most rickety, collapsible piece of wood ever tacked together. *Why in the world didn't he buy a table instead of a table cloth?* "Do you have meals at this table?" I asked. "Gosh no", my friend answered. "You're standing closer to it than we usually get. I just wanted you to see my new tablecloth."

I thanked him for his invitation and commented absently that it was a very elaborate and beautiful tablecloth. I'd never seen anything like it.

This is the way I feel about our country. We keep proclaiming bold initiatives to procure a more beautiful tablecloth when our problem is we need a new table. What lies underneath is what needs repair or replacement. A flood is coming; a flood of problems the magnitude of which we have never experienced. What will be our testimony? Will we have built an ark of safety, a faith that endures through the shaking that lies before us?

Will we embrace both the mercy and the judgment of the Lord? Allow the blood of Jesus to cover us completely and in doing so make us solid from top to bottom. "My dear brothers and sisters, stand firm. Let nothing move you. Always give yourselves fully to the work of the Lord, because you know that your labor in the Lord is not in vain." (I Corinthians 15: 58)

Study Questions:

1.   Do you think most people go about their business because they believe judgment day (if there is such a thing) is a long way off or they live like they do because they believe judgment is near at hand?

2.   How do you go about daily embracing or seeking the truth? What does a life look like when it resists the truth? Are there any identifying signs or markers?

3.   Why is it easier to fictionalize or mythologize the battle of good and evil than it is to have a fact-based conversation about it? Do we want to be a part of a bigger story if we are an actual part? How do we forsake the real idols we have?

4.   What would it take for us to persevere in our faith when the whole world says we're crazy? Could we build an ark if God asked us?

The Big IF

"If my people, who are called by my name, will humble themselves and pray and seek my face and turn from their wicked ways, then will I hear from heaven and will forgive their sin and will heal their land."

(2nd Chronicles 14)

Want to watch our grandbaby get excited and laugh out loud? All I have to do is tell her I am coming to get her. She may try to run but I head her off at the pass. She may try to juke and jive and run from side to side but I mirror her movements, only I'm faster. I've been at this a whole lot longer than she has. I swoop in for the squeal, the lift, and the hug. Then I get all the sugars I can as she laughs out loud with delight.

This is the image I have of God's pursuit of us. What about you? If you knew the Lord was coming to get you would you become excited and laugh out loud with joy and delight? We saw in the last chapter the whole point of God's goodness is to bring us to a place of repentance. The reason why there are noticeable signs of the time is so we can have ample opportunity to get our divided house in order. If the Lord is always leading us to victory and "victory loves preparation", (Suetonius, Life of Titus 8.1) then the "big if" is, will we prepare for the victory into which God wants to lead us?

If My People Called by My Name

Are you one of God's people? Do you have the witness of the Holy Spirit within you that you are a child of God? I know God has called you to a life rooted in his grace and truth. Have you responded to that call? This is the "Big IF"! Will you follow the pathway of grace for your life or will you remain rooted in your own nature, missing the mark for what you were created. Romans 8: 28 says "And we know that in all things God works for the good of those who love him, who have been called according to his purpose."

Note when we are God's people we love God and are those called according to his purpose or name. It is furthering God's brand or kingdom that animates us and pulls us forward. Do you get it? When God calls you it is a positive development in your life. Listen to Jesus as he begins his ministry of calling people to follow him. "Repent, for the kingdom of heaven is near." (Matthew 3: 2) There is no condemnation: "Repent because you are a sinner and going to hell." Jesus doesn't say that. Everyone who wasn't an uppity SOB knew that left to themselves it was a foregone conclusion that they would split hell wide open. It was only the proud in heart, those who thought of themselves as perfectly fine, who had a false confidence of heaven.

This is why the gospel writer of Mark makes it even more emphatic the point of Jesus' call. "The time has come," he said. "The kingdom of God is near. Repent and believe the good news!" (Mark 1: 15) Jesus is the good news. Jesus alone, crucified, buried, and risen, offers any of us an open heaven and a closed hell. We have all sinned. The result of sin is death. The result of death is judgment. The result of judgment is determined by your response to God's call.

Everything is set in motion for your good when you turn to Jesus Christ. This is not optional. Jesus speaks to those who believe they are entitled to heaven when he describes them as wicked and adulterous. (Matthew 12: 39, 16: 4) They seek after signs, secrets, and special reasons why they should need to repent. It is not enough that Jesus has suffered or laid down his life for them, the innocent bearing the penalty of the guilty. It is not enough that Jesus rose from the grave, triumphing over death and opening a way of life for all who believe in him as Lord. No, they require more.

C. S. Lewis says "Of all tyrannies, a tyranny sincerely exercised for the good of its victims may be the most oppressive." (God in the Dock: Essays on Theology & Ethics, Eerdmans Publishing Company, 1994) This tyranny is especially gruesome for those who victimize themselves through unbelief and a willful lack of repentance. They count themselves morally obligated to hold to the fool's dogma that grace is the entitlement of the breathing and they miss the most important aspect of grace and the life it affords – grace is a gift.

Today is the day to receive that gift if you haven't already. If you have received the gift of God you know what comes next.

Humble Themselves

To be those called by God's name is to know something of God's presence prior to judgment day. God meets us where we are in the way. God chooses us, we don't choose him. Any self-directed pursuit of God's kingdom is bound to fail. Every person must come into the kingdom through the door of repentance. God's call opens the door and self-direction must and will be commanded to turn itself in before you will be allowed to go further

The *Big IF* demands a response and that response must be a humble one. Jesus will give no encouragement to your pride. He will not egg on your ego. He will ask of you the very same thing he asks of us all: "Then he said to them all: 'If anyone would come after me, he must deny himself and take up his cross daily and follow me'." (Luke 9: 23)

When a young man tried to volunteer to follow Jesus, the response Jesus gave was not "You're welcome." Jesus did not applaud the man for his choice or for having what it took to be a good follower. "As they were walking along the road, a man said to him, 'I will follow you wherever you go.' Jesus replied, 'Foxes have holes and birds of the air have nests, but the Son of Man has no place to lay his head.' He said to another man, 'Follow me.' But the man replied, 'Lord, first let me go and bury my father.' Jesus said to him, 'Let the dead bury their own dead, but you go and proclaim the kingdom of God.' Still another said, 'I will follow you, Lord; but first let me go back and say good-by to my family.' Jesus replied, 'No one who puts his hand to the plow and looks back is fit for service in the kingdom of God'." (Luke 9: 57 – 62)

The time to be humble before God is not up to you and me. We don't walk up to God on our schedule and tell God I'm ready to go. God comes to us and the call is given. Leave everything and go or we're carrying too much baggage to pass through the straight and narrow gate that leads to life.

What does it mean to be humble? It means to be brought low. It means as we will see in our next section to be brought to our knees in prayer. Humility with God is the only thing that can help us stand uprightly before others. Humility echoes the seven core values of the U. S. Army: loyalty, duty, respect, selfless service, honor, integrity, and personal courage.

Humility is the self-surrender of a soul entrusting itself into the hands of God. It is not the disposition of a wimp but the true nature of a warrior. We are becoming the instruments of God's grace, weapons he wields to pour out his mercy. As a weapon humility insures we are completely broken down for cleaning and use by the Master Warrior. Humility allows God to cleanse us completely of the gunk left in our system by sin. Humility welcomes the oil of God's anointing and power. We trust the Lord to reassemble us into the image of his Son. Humility provides the restraint necessary to keep us from reasserting our way before the Lord's.

But, how does a nation humble itself? It has representatives call for repentance and works that are appropriate for a repenting people. From where do these representatives arise? They arise from the seven spheres, or mountains of society that are the pillars of any society. These seven mountains are business, government, media, arts and entertainment, education, the family and religion. In 1975, Bill Bright, founder of Campus Crusade, and Loren Cunningham, founder of Youth With a Mission, had lunch together in Colorado. God simultaneously gave each of these change agents a message to give to the other. During that same time frame Francis Schaeffer was given a similar message. What was the *Big IF*? If we are to impact any nation for Jesus Christ, leading men and women within these areas of influence would live and move called by God's name and they would humble themselves appropriately to share in a vision of grace and freedom. (http://www.reclaim7mountains.com/)

Are we humbling ourselves before the Lord? Are we being faithful to God's calling?

Pray

The way humility gains momentum in our lives is through prayer. Imagine yourself as a paint roller. God has you in his hand and there is a place he wants to change or brighten. The act of prayer is the act of rolling you, turning you to receive the paint. Yes, you cannot operate as you were intended without the paint being all over you but in the back of your mind you know the reason you are being covered and saturated is so you can affect something beyond yourself.

To pray is to be called to God's way of looking at things. Everything we face is judged by God's steamrolling effect upon us. Every opinion we hold is brought even with God's word. Every feeling or emotion is worked out under the influence of God's presence and Holy Spirit. Just as the sheep is anointed with oil by deeply rubbing and working the oil into the skin sheared of its wool, God is working his ways into the thoughts and intentions of our heart in prayer.

If we do not pray, we do not expose the skin of our soul to God's anointing. With no skin in the game, we will gravitate towards whatever is most popular or whatever is the most convenient, leave-me-out-of the hard-stuff, solutions that people offer for the problems of the day.

Jesus aims to keep us from this trap when he teaches us how to pray. His admonition begins with a deep call to repentance and holiness, "Our Father in heaven, hallowed be your name". (Matthew 6: 9) That is then echoed back with a self-sacrificing faith, "your kingdom come, your will be done on earth as it is in heaven." (Matthew 6: 10) "Give us today our daily bread" (Matthew 6: 11) reminds us we can trust God to prescribe for us what we need each day. The provision of God allows for us to be at our entrepreneurial best. We can step up for others because we know God will step up for us. And, though our ways may not be perfect, our systems seem unfair at times, there is forgiveness and the power to correct or amend our ways as we go. "Forgive us our debts, as we also have forgiven our debtors." (Matthew 6: 12)

Be careful how you pray. God's way of praying leads us to forgive those who we believe owe us or others. The devil's way of praying leads us to force those who owe us to owe more. It will request that more tests and regulations be established to make people pay their fair share. The devil's way will call for men to be humbled. God's way will call on them to become his and as his people to humble themselves, pray, seek his face and turn from their wicked ways.

Be careful how you pray because when you do you are intervening and interposing your faith into the lives of others. This is the awesome power and responsibility we have by grace in prayer. Jesus counsels us to pray "lead us not into temptation". (Matthew 6: 13a) Why? Jesus knows we naturally turn away from what puts us to the test. God wants us to turn away from our wicked ways not from our obligations. Yes, there are times when men must be forced to face their obligations, such as garnishing wages to secure child support but we all agree it would be better if parents did this freely and voluntarily. So, the last phrase of the prayer is offered: "deliver us from the evil one." (Matthew 6: 13b) Deliver us from the one who steals, kills, and destroys and says that theft, murder, and destruction are all for the greater good. Deliver us from the liar who lies because they know best how to set us free. Deliver us from seeking anything but the face of God.

Deliver us and let us pray.

Seek My Face

The writing is there. We call it braille. Sensitive fingers can tell you what it says. Are you one of God's people, called by his name? Are you humble? Do you pray? Your prayers can give the sense to your soul to read what God writes on your heart. Searching after God's will, you will find a ready response from God. "If any of you lacks wisdom, he should ask God, who gives generously to all without finding fault, and it will be given to him." (James 1: 5)

God is willing to turn to you, see you where you are, and enter into a relationship with you. Even when others try to dissuade you and tell you prayer is an impotent religious gesture God is encouraging you to draw near.

Turn from Their Wicked Ways

In a recent fundraising trip to New York, the president quietly stopped off at Ground Zero to pay his respects and to write words that are meant to be encouraging, perhaps even inspirational on a steel girder: "We remember. We rebuild. We come back stronger." But, what do these words really portend? Do they give us hope for the future or are they a tribute to our unwillingness to turn to God and turn from our wicked ways?

The Super Bowl commercial began with these words: "It's Halftime in America. And our second half is about to begin. All that matters now is looking ahead and finding a way forward." But, that's not all that matters. What if you come out in the second half and do the same stupid things you did in the first half? How can you expect to win repeating what made you a loser in the first place?

It was obvious. The Chrysler sponsored ad with Clint Eastwood's voiced over content was the best produced commercial of Super Bowl XLVI but it was a total farce and a lie. The ad was meant to use Detroit as representative of the comeback America would experience but most of the footage came from Los Angeles and New Orleans.

Look at the president's words again: "We remember. We rebuild. We come back stronger." Remembering is a good thing, right? Yes, if in remembering you do more than remember the pain of the event and vow now to feel that again. I cracked my ankle one time and before it was healed tried to run on it. What was the result? My ankle broke. The doctors said my ankle had not been broken. The x-rays didn't show anything. The diagnosis they gave: a chronic sprain. With a little help the natural resiliency of my ankle would return so I was sent to rehab.

But, my ankle was broken. Rehab only caused me more pain. Surgery nine months after the painful event removed the broken bone and I have been on my way to good-to-go ever since. No amount of rehab or stimulation could have returned my ankle to its natural resiliency. In the same way our nation is broken and no amount of rehab, stimulation, or monetization of our problems will return us to a 'stronger second half'. It will only delay the inevitable surgery that is needed and bring us more pain.

I encourage you to read Jonathan Cahn's book, Harbinger. There you will find a more detailed explanation of how America is trying to rehab itself rather than turn from its wicked ways. One way brings healing; the other, only more pain. What will we do?

Then, I Will Hear from Heaven and...

I can still remember it. R2D2 is projecting an image of Princess Leia transmitting a message to someone name Obi wan Kenobi. The message is urgent and top secret. Luke, our hero-in-waiting hears the words replayed, "Help us Obi wan. You're our only hope." This is a turning point in the saga we call Star Wars. Once, Luke sets out to find 'Old Ben' Kenobi, his journey is forever changed.

Our nation stands at a similar point of faith. Will we see the signs of the time and join with others to humble ourselves before the Lord? Will we cry out together, "Help us, Lord; you're our only hope." Will this be the first breath of our prayers? Will we seek the face of God? Will that be the hidden treasure that motivates our actions and keeps our hearts in love and peace? Will we turn from our wicked ways?

Will the world and the greater majority of people help us in this? I think you know the answer to that question. Will the media begin to exalt Jesus and favor the gospel above other news they could report? You and I both know a wreck is more attention grabbing than a work of restoration. Which would get the headline – craftsman restores vintage piece of furniture or man throws desk out of office window?

The world is set against us. Why? It cannot be preserved and purified at the same time. Those who seek power in this age have to immunize themselves against eternal measures. They do not or cannot care about our souls. We are consumers, random polling data, fodder for their ambition and profit. They do not know our name except as an encrypted digital piece of code. They can promise hope and change but the scriptures say the promise of hope and glory rest in the fact Christ is in us. (Colossians 1: 27) Outside of this, our hopes are all fleeting and subject to the next political wind that blows.

We desire a relationship with the living God. So, Lord, have mercy. Initiate the threefold breakthrough sequence that ignites revival and restoration to our nation and to each person who wants to walk before you.

What is that breakthrough sequence? It is the compression of God's grace into three movements that transform our lives and forestall judgment. It is a sequence of repentance and faith, prayer and longing, turning and receiving. It holds no animosity or defiance towards God. It desires no separation or distance. It is not wise in its own eyes but is content to live by every word that proceeds from the mouth of God.

Study Questions:

1. Where are you the strongest and most comfortable on the threefold breakthrough sequence? Where do you come up short?

2. Are we humbling ourselves before the Lord? Are we being faithful to God's calling?

3. On a scale of 1 to 10 how is your prayer life? How consistent is it? How constant is it? How fervent is it? How scripturally based is it?

4. How do you seek God's face? Scripture reading? Fasting? Prayer? Reflection? Corporate worship? Small group confession or sharing? Stillness? How do you seek after God's presence?

5. In our spiritual warfare, what are the hindrances to healing for ourselves and our land?

6. Where have you experienced or seen evidence of revival or renewal? What are you doing to move towards it?

What Do You Know?

God is our refuge and strength, an ever-present help in trouble. Therefore we will not fear, though the earth give way and the mountains fall into the heart of the sea, though its waters roar and foam and the mountains quake with their surging. Selah. There is a river whose streams make glad the city of God, the holy place where the Most High dwells. God is within her, she will not fall; God will help her at break of day. Nations are in uproar, kingdoms fall; he lifts his voice, the earth melts. The LORD Almighty is with us; the God of Jacob is our fortress. Selah. Come and see the works of the LORD, the desolations he has brought on the earth. He makes wars cease to the ends of the earth; he breaks the bow and shatters the spear, he burns the shields with fire. "Be still, and know that I am God; I will be exalted among the nations, I will be exalted in the earth." The LORD Almighty is with us; the God of Jacob is our fortress. Selah. (Psalm 46)

Do you know God? Do you know God as your refuge and strength, "an ever-present help in time of trouble"? Do you know how to call on God and hear from God when everything and everyone is roaring around you?

Can You See the Works of God?

Have you ever seen someone correct their child? It is uncomfortable even if you know the child was disobedient and disrespectful. It is uncomfortable even when the child was endangering himself or herself. Correction feels inappropriate. The Psalmist describes the corrections as desolations. The Psalmist calls us to see them for what they really are: an invitation to be still before God and exalt him above everything else. The word 'see' in Hebrew implies that we are to become preoccupied with the works of God. Like me (and most guys) in front of a television, we are open mouthed, zoned in, and blocking everything else out. Others may try to get our attention. Others may try to tell us there is something else going on but we only have eyes for what we see in front of us. The Psalmist here is asking us to set the works of God before us and fix our eyes on them.

He Makes Wars to Cease

We are at war with God and each other. God is committed to winning that war. God is committed to prevailing and bringing us to a place of triumph.

Have you ever watched the program on A & E called *Hoarders*? It is an uncomfortable show to watch. People are drowning in their own purchases. They are paralyzed and imprisoned in the avalanche of specials that have become trash. Good deals have accumulated and become a great deal of unnecessary and stifling stuff. Know now, God is committed to refining our lives, giving us clarity and focus about what is essential and important.

The first of the desolations God brings upon a person and a nation is he makes wars or consumption to cease. With every war there is carnage and waste. With every war there are squandered opportunities and resources. Every day there are billion dollar wars between nations and tyrants, between regulatory controls and free people, between patience and impatience, between fear and faith-filled opportunity. In the midst of our life as a consumer, will we hear the clarion call to "seek first the kingdom of heaven and its righteousness"? (Matthew 6: 33)

God Breaks the Bow

God bursts our bubbles. It is a commitment God carries out to fulfill His word: "You reap what you sow." Thus, if God initiates anything in our lives God will watch over his word to perform it. But, if Jesus is not the author of something, Jesus is also not the finisher of it. Yes, Jesus can and does redeem us from our trouble but he never doubles down on sin so that grace can abound.

Bubbles are everywhere. The most important is the faith bubble. Jesus is concerned and warns us of the danger of a dissipating faith, a faith that pops and deflates when dryness, hardship, or the wind of trouble blows against us. He even asks the question: "when the Son of Man comes, will he find faith on the earth?" (Luke 18: 8)

There are also a host of other bubbles. The housing bubble. The commercial real estate bubble. The debt bubble. The food supply bubble. The water bubble. The energy bubble. The derivatives bubble. The currency bubble. Our problem is they all seem ready to burst. Will the earthquake of my dream shake our fragile exterior into bursting? Will the threat of war put pressure on our bubble?

We all have bubbles. What's that? It is our personal situation we are trying to rectify that we want no one to mess up. If the country is going to collapse let it be right after I finish fixing my stuff, after I get my house in order. If the health services and insurance bubble is going to be obliterated by Obamacare let me first get my situation secured. Our bubble is our peculiar brand of selfishness or concern. It is the 800 pound gorilla. It is the elephant in the room of our common conversation. Cut whatever needs to be cut except the programs and aid that benefits me.

Bubbles will burst. The kingdom of God will burst through them. The consequences of sin will blow them up. In a new book Terence Jeffrey says this is *Totally Predictable* whether we are talking about earthly things or heavenly things. "A nation whose government spends per family more than the typical family earns is on the road to ruin." In just ten years the government has gone from spending $12,049 less than the median household income to $629 more on average than the median household income. This happened while the median household income rose by $7,500. When government spends more than the governed make can that bubble be sustained?

God breaks the bow. That is a declaration of fact. God bursts the bubble except the bubble that is wet with the truth and power of God's presence. This is why we maintain our hope. We know God can pour out the Holy Spirit to govern our affairs and forestall judgment. The nature of bubbles shows us that. When the air is full of moisture, bubbles will seemingly last forever. This is why we seek God's face for revival. The bubbles may burst but we will endure to the very end.

God Shatters the Spear

We have propped ourselves up on the almighty dollar and that prop is about to be kicked out from under us. America has relied upon her military might but this prop, too, is about to be pulled out from under us.

We will soon be trying to exist on a yard sale economy. What do I mean? Well, you've been to a yard sale, haven't you? No matter how valuable your possessions no one wants to give you anything for them. My mama once bought me an official NFL-licensed Miami Dolphin, black leather jacket at a yard sale. Being a big Dolphin's fan I was excited to receive it. I asked Mama how much she had paid for it. I had seen something with a little less quality on the internet for around a hundred and fifty dollars. Mama said, "He wanted five dollars for it but I told him it was a yard sale and he let me have it for three."

Now, imagine we're talking about your checking account. Last week you used your debit card to buy a few groceries: milk, butter, eggs, and sausage for your breakfast. This set you back for a little over ten dollars. But, what happens as inflation or hyperinflation kicks in? Suddenly, you're spending twelve instead of ten; then when you go back it's fifteen or twenty. Don't think it's possible? It is. Study your history. Look at the Weimar Republic of Germany. Don't think anything that happened that long ago has any bearing on today? Well, look at Zimbabwe in the last decade. My grocery example is far too modest in describing what hyperinflation could mean. Let me quote from a New York Times article by Michael Wines in May 2006, entitled, *How Bad is Inflation in Zimbabwe?*

> HARARE, Zimbabwe, April 25 — How bad is inflation in Zimbabwe? Well, consider this: at a supermarket near the center of this tatterdemalion capital, toilet paper costs $417.
>
> No, not per roll. Four hundred seventeen Zimbabwean dollars is the value of a single two-ply sheet. A roll costs $145,750 — in American currency, about 69 cents.
>
> The price of toilet paper, like everything else here, soars almost daily, spawning jokes about an impending better use for Zimbabwe's $500 bill, now the smallest in circulation.
>
> But what is happening is no laughing matter. For untold numbers of Zimbabweans, toilet paper — and bread, margarine, meat, even the once ubiquitous morning cup of tea — have become unimaginable luxuries. All are casualties of the hyperinflation that is roaring toward 1,000 percent a year, a rate usually seen only in war zones.
>
> Zimbabwe has been tormented this entire decade by both deep recession and high inflation, but in recent months the economy

seems to have abandoned whatever moorings it had left. The national budget for 2006 has already been largely spent. Government services have started to crumble.

The article goes on to describe the daily horrors of living beneath this kind of inflationary pressure. What were the primary reasons Zimbabwe devolved into this mess? The three reasons given in a correction printed a month after the original article, were "a flight of foreign capital, shortages and a steep increase in the money supply."

All three of these could be seen as applicable to the economics of the United States. We are presently experiencing a flight from our capital markets, so much so that the Federal Reserve is currently buying 61% of the government debt issued by the United States Treasury according to a Wall Street Journal report by Julie Crawshaw and Forrest Jones cited at www.moneynews.com on March 28, 2012. Lawrence Goodman, a former Treasury official and current president of the Center for Financial Stability, says it is "a trend that cannot last." Goodman goes on to say, "This not only creates the false appearance of limitless demand for U.S. debt but also blunts any sense of urgency to reduce supersized budget deficits." "A sharp correction" is coming, Goodman warned.

Have we heeded the warning? Not yet, we haven't. We have tried to hide the flight of capital and shop around the shortages that we have experienced due to drought and disaster. We have ample fuel reserves of all kinds but we are limiting access or opportunity to a great deal of those. We continue to push solutions off into the future because they won't be realized until sometime in the future. Duh! Follow that logic and I can't write this section of the book today because the rest of the book can't be finished until later.

Oh, and if you thought the third reason for hyperinflation, an increase in the money supply, didn't apply to us; you would be wrong. That is the invisible elephant in the room. QE3, the third round of quantitative easing, has already begun. What are its effects? Well, some say it helps to keep interest rates low but that means our future is being cut off in spite of our present. Think about Social Security. You pay in your whole working life but can you count on it for your future? No, you can't. And, the reason is not because the government has already spent the money. The reason is because a low interest rate for loans also translates into lower interest rates for investment income. In other words, from the get go of your retirement you'll be shrinking your principle. Even low inflation will trump non-existent interest every time.

Doesn't this printing and loaning of money help the economy? You decide. Is it effective help if you spend about $90,000 to make a $30,000 job? If you think that is good for the economy and you can't foresee any problem with that method of job creation, remind me not to get financial advice from you.

But, what is the inevitable worst result of the increase in money supply? It is the devaluing of our dollar and the inflation that has to follow. God says this is a step we can see coming. Right after the bubble bursts, he "shatters the spear" (Psalm 46: 9), God kicks the props out.

Will we repent of our hollow prop of printing and spending what we do not have? Will we repent of borrowing tomorrow for today? This is not an easy repentance. So many would have their lives as they know it shattered if we repented as a nation. I know from personal experience paying for the credit card after you quit using it is a whole lot more painful than the guilt of running it up in the first place.

Yet, I am here to testify there is hope in the midst of the pain. Our current national debt of over 16 trillion comes to $53, 378 per person (November 2012, Minority Report, Senate Budget Committee). That means for me and my house to share in the nation's repentance, I would have to be responsible for covering that. You would take responsibility for your share and so on down the line. We couldn't blame others even though we didn't personally spend any of the money. We would make arrangements with our representatives that we will not stand for accumulating further debt. We cannot prop ourselves up on a lie. We don't want to wait for a 16+ trillion dollar shoe to drop on our nation or continue to be saddled with an additional $250 debt obligation every month on every person in the country.

He Burns the Shields with Fire

Did you know God consumes what consumes us? That is the essence of this verse. God does not allow for idolatry to endure. It can't anyway. Jesus guards us against this 'work' or judgment of God when he says, "Do not store up for yourselves treasures on earth, where moth and rust destroy, and where thieves break in and steal. But store up for yourselves, treasures in heaven, where moth and rust do not destroy, and where thieves do not break in and steal. For where your treasure is, there your heart will be also." (Matthew 6: 19 – 21)

Proverbs chapter one warns us too of the danger of tagging along with sinners on their dead end pursuits. "These men lie in wait for their own blood; they waylay only themselves! Such is the end of all who go after ill-gotten gain; it takes away the lives of those who get it." (Proverbs 1: 18 – 19) A human being, a righteous person is meant to have a revolving and evolving relationship with the living God; not be like flies, swarming around a corpse.

Do as the hymn, Rise Up, O Men of God says: "Rise up, O men of God! Have done with lesser things. Give heart and mind and soul and strength to serve the King of kings."

Be Still and Know

Hopefully, you've been here before, to this place of stillness. This is the final preparation. This is the place of extreme watchfulness that breaks through into extreme worship. What does it look like in nature? It is the rabbit perfectly still, ears on high alert, waiting for its instincts to tell it to dash towards its refuge. It is the deer ready to spring into action, moving forward to a place of hightailing it to safety.

Being still and knowing God is your call to see that map or first set of directions from the map from God that leads to deliverance. We allow our spirit to be commended to the Holy Spirit.

You've seen it in the scripture when Moses and the nation stand before the Sea and Pharoah with his army is bearing down on them. The command is given, "Do not be afraid. Stand firm and you will see the deliverance the LORD will bring you today. The Egyptians you see today you will never see again. The LORD will fight for you; you need only to be still."(Exodus 14: 13 – 14) The standard of stillness is exalted and then notice what God says about that! "Then the LORD said to Moses, "Why are you crying out to me? Tell the Israelites to move on." (Exodus 14: 15) This is the miracle of redeeming grace. We will know how to move forward after we have come to a place of stillness before the Lord.

See Joshua preparing the next generation to cross the Jordan into the Promised Land. Their feet are required to step forward to see what the Lord will do. It is after the feet are placed in the water bearing the Ark of the Lord that the waters begin to get pushed back into a heap upstream.

This is the prepper's resolve. It is the martyr's peace. It is the witness' final revelation. Revelation describes it as "the patience of the saints". It is the heart of Daniel who earnestly sought and practiced coming to this place of stillness that brought him safe through the Lion's Den. It is the fidelity to their faith and principles that bring Shadrach, Meshach, and Abednego to and through the fiery furnace with the fourth man in the fire by their side.

This is Jesus in the garden of the wine press, in Gethsemane, where he says, "Not my will, but yours be done." Are you there, yet? Don't fret if you don't think so. You see, the most important aspect of this stillness is not you being fixed and ready to do what is required. It is having your eyes "looking unto Jesus the author and finisher of [our] faith; who for the joy that was set before him endured the cross, despising the shame, and is set down at the right hand of the throne of God. For consider him that endured such contradiction of sinners against himself, lest ye be wearied and faint in your minds." (Hebrews 12: 2-3)

You are not alone. There are others, your brothers and sisters of faith, who are also fixing their eyes on the exalted Jesus. Stand with them. It doesn't necessarily mean the end has come. Perhaps it is more the end to you and me and our preoccupation with self.

This stillness is not the quiet rage and determination of pride. It is the calm assurance of humility. This is the dependent cry of Jacob in the wilderness. It is not the Isaiah 9: 10 repetition of defiance as we heard from New York Governor Andrew Cuomo after the Hurricane Sandy disaster. Commenting on reconstructing our reconstructions, he said, "This is the Ground Zero site. This is a monument to human capacity and human endurance. And, this is New Yorkers' way of saying we're not going to give up. We're going to come back and we will. This city will rebuild and the state will rebuild, and I believe will be the better for it."

It doesn't matter what nature or nature's God throws at us, we can choose stillness or stubbornness. Which will our nation choose? What will you choose?

Study Questions:

1. How have you experienced correction in your life? How did you receive it? Was it welcomed? Was it received reluctantly or under protest? Was it resented? Rejected? How have you experienced the Lord's correction in your life? What made it different or was it?

2. In what ways if any have you had to cut back your consumption of things? Are there areas of your life that would benefit from that kind of contraction? Are there areas of your life that have been hurt by this kind of contraction?

3. Can you name the bubbles in your life? How are you working within them? How are you preparing for the day when bubbles burst?

4. What kind of devotional props do you use: the Bible, devotional apps, music, small groups? How do they help you in your walk with God? What if they were lost? How would you still grow in your relationship with God?

5. What if the props get kicked out from under our economy? How would you still be a good neighbor and a faithful disciple?

6. How do you keep still when everything around you is shaking? How is God exalted in your life? How do you sense that "The LORD Almighty is with us; the God of Jacob is our fortress"?

The Lord's Prayer

Such being the impressions under which I have, in obedience to the public summons, repaired to the present station, it would be peculiarly improper to omit in this first official act my fervent supplications to that Almighty Being who rules over the universe, who presides in the councils of nations, and whose providential aids can supply every human defect, that His benediction may consecrate to the liberties and happiness of the people of the United States a Government instituted by themselves for these essential purposes, and may enable every instrument employed in its administration to execute with success the functions allotted to his charge. In tendering this homage to the Great Author of every public and private good, I assure myself that it expresses your sentiments not less than my own, nor those of my fellow-citizens at large less than either. No people can be bound to acknowledge and adore the Invisible Hand which conducts the affairs of men more than those of the United States. Every step by which they have advanced to the character of an independent nation seems to have been distinguished by some token of providential agency; and in the important revolution just accomplished in the system of their united government the tranquil deliberations and voluntary consent of so many distinct communities from which the event has resulted cannot be compared with the means by which most governments have been established without some return of pious gratitude, along with an humble anticipation of the future blessings which the past seem to presage. These reflections, arising out of the present crisis, have forced themselves too strongly on my mind to be suppressed. You will join with me, I trust, in thinking that there are none under the influence of which the proceedings of a new and free government can more auspiciously commence.

George Washington, First
Inaugural Address

"Unless you repent, you too will all perish."

Luke 13: 3 & 5

There are hundreds, if not thousands of examples of prayers given by leaders that call for us to trust the Lord, to acknowledge God's divine providence, and to give God the tribute for blessings past, present, and future. Sadly, most of those examples are from another time other than our own. Too often today, God is a token or vain name we use to validate our own agenda and acts of defiance.

Even among those who claim knowledge of the Lord, I believe many are stuck in a second hand faith. What do I mean? I believe many acquaint knowledge of the church and church people with a relationship with God. Think about it this way. You have a friend. You've been friends for years. You meet with each other regularly. You talk together and on occasion that conversation has centered on your friend's spouse. You have never gotten to know him. You were introduced once but it was only in passing.

You believe you know him because you know his spouse. She speaks of him regularly. You know what he likes and doesn't like. You know what he does each day. You get the sense he really loves your friend and that if you spent time with him you would experience a deep sense of friendship with him. But, if someone asked her husband does he know you, he would have to say, "Not really. They're a friend of my bride."

This is the picture the scripture paints of the judgment when God says "I never knew you; depart from me." (Matthew 7: 23) The judgment is not determined by how much you know about God but how much God has been free to know about you. Have you given yourself to God as a bride gives herself to her husband or have you been content to be a friend of the bride who finds it inappropriate or distasteful to think about a relationship more intimate than that? You follow the Bette Midler song and let God operate "from a distance".

God wants to have an intimate walk with you. The Bible says it is only with the proud and the unbelieving that God is put in a position of operating at a distance. Have you kept yourself from God? Has your sin separated you from the Lord? Jesus offers you one of many invitations to close that gap. Choose one and move in faith to respond.

> "Come and you will see." (John 1: 39)

> "Let anyone who is thirsty come to me and drink." (John 7: 37)

> "Come to me, all you who are weary and burdened, and I will give you rest." (Matthew 11: 28)

> "Then he said to them all: 'Whoever wants to be my disciple must deny themselves and take up their cross daily and follow me'." (Luke 9: 23)

The Lord's Prayer for you is you will know God intimately. You can say of the Lord's purpose for your life: "You had my curiosity but now you have my attention." (Leonardo DiCaprio as Calvin Candie in Django Unchained) Yes, the Lord's Prayer for you is to be enthralled by the Father's love, filled with his joy, and held steadfast in his peace. The Lord's Prayer for you is that your faith and confidence will be great, partners together with God in healing and in the working of miracles. The Lord's Prayer for you is you will be a prophetic person in God's kingdom, sharing out loud what you hear from the Lord up close and personal.

Hallowed Be Thy Name

It is difficult to sanctify something from a distance. It almost always requires proximity, either inward or outward. You can sanctify something for the future from a distance, like reserving a plane ticket or reservation online, but it is not truly set apart as yours until you stand at the counter or with the ticket agent and say this is mine. In order to sanctify God in your heart, God must have an intimate or proximate place in your experience.

What happens in you when you are away from God? Do you miss Him? Recently my granddaughter spent some time with other family members. We were only away from each other for a few days but when we were apart my heart ached to break free of my rib cage and be with her. Is there a yearning in you like that for God? I can hardly describe the excitement and joy of getting back together with each other.

This is the choice of each person, each community, and nation. Psalm 33: 12 says, "Blessed is the nation whose God is the Lord; the people he chose for his inheritance." The Bible says, "Taste and see that the Lord is good." In the old westerns, they would bite down on a gold coin to see if it was legitimate. You bit it to see if your teeth would put a dent in it or not. If the coin was something harder than gold and you could make no mark on it, it is a fake. If it's only gold layered over something, you bit through the gold and found out what you really have.

As a nation, a daily sampling or tasting of the Lord is rare. We are surprised when a public school child learns to sing a song of praise and faith. Even sadder, we forbid the public revelation of the holy or obscure it behind secular expressions. Saddest of all is when we don't teach our children in a Christian context to honor God.

I am thankful my two year old granddaughter knows about the rain coming down as we are "building up the temple for the Lord" as well as when it falls and washes the 'itsy-bitsy spider' down the waterspout.

Look around. Are there places where we have forsaken the praise of God and have become unfamiliar with it? Are there places where it is despised and fought against? This is why the first breath of prayer and the first hope of a nation begins the way Jesus teaches us to pray. "Our Father in heaven, hallowed be your name." (Matthew 6: 9)

We cannot be talking about some static national identity. It does us no good to be considered a Christian nation, have all the forms correct but deny the power and presence of God in our lives. No, the Lord's Prayer insists that the respect we give to the Lord is no patriotic obligation but a personal and pervasive relationship we have with the One whose name is Holy. God wants us to realize the One who inhabits eternity must inhabit a very real place in our heart and soul.

A friend of mine went with a friend to a breakfast political meeting recently. As folks around them mixed and mingled they sat down at a table in preparation for the meal to come. My friend's friend gently asked the others at the table if they might return thanks for their food and time together. With no one objecting, he offered a brief acknowledgement to God for the provision and blessing of the day.

My friend said the others at the table were all open-mouthed and aghast, asking if her friend was a preacher. He isn't. They self-defensively tried to assert their faith or affiliation while admitting they never would have thought to pray in this kind of setting. They again pressed my friend's friend with a question, "Are you a minister of some kind?" He replied "We are all ministers."

This is the latent call within the Lord's Prayer. If you hallow his name you are one of his ministers. "We are therefore Christ's ambassadors" (2 Corinthians 5: 20) the Apostle Paul tells the church in Corinth. And I tell you, if you hallow the name of God, if you have a relationship with God Our Father, you become privy to some marvelous good news. "Therefore, if anyone is in Christ, the new creation has come: The old has gone, the new is here! All this is from God, who reconciled us to himself through

Christ and gave us the ministry of reconciliation: that God was reconciling the world to himself in Christ, not counting people's sins against them. And he has committed to us the message of reconciliation." (2 Corinthians 5: 17 – 19)

This good news and the ministry to which it includes us is not something for which we are ashamed or defensive. It makes us glad. It brings us peace and confidence. It elevates our standard of behavior and our level of appreciation.

I am asking you to get with the program. Initiate and form a habit of sanctifying the Lord in your heart, of coming into the presence of "Our Father, in heaven, hallowed be your name." (Matthew 6: 9) Without this alignment of repentance your witness will be more than diminished; it will be skewed out of phase. As my good friend Jean Holmes taught me, "You can't have a witness until you first get a with-ness!"

Without this 'with-ness' with the Father eventually you will oppose God and make Him your enemy. God will be an interrupter of your plans. You will consider God rude, not kind. In every way I Corinthians 13 describes God as Love, you will experience the opposite. God will be impatient, always asking you to repent. God will not be kind; you'll feel as if he is mean and petty and never satisfied with you. God will be small in your eyes, envious and jealous of your independence and potential. You will become rivals rather than friends. Instead of going from glory to glory, you will move from one disagreement and dispute to another. You will be asked to swallow your way for his. Always wondering, *should I pull out of this relationship I don't really have*?

How can I say this? How can I make this assertion? I know the nature and pathway of sin. I know sin has a one-track way of doing things and every step of that path sets out to steal, kill, and destroy your with-ness with God. This is why I have felt compelled to include this chapter on the Lord's Prayer. America, we need to learn how to pray. We need to get a with-ness with God. It is our only hope. The alternative is enmity with God and receiving the consequences of being a nation pierced.

Your Kingdom Come, Your Will Be Done

It's a simple prayer. Let my life be something bigger than me sucking wind for however many years I am resident on the earth. John Ruskin said, "When a man is wrapped up in himself, he makes a pretty small package." So, if life is a gift return the favor. Let's make our life bigger, more valuable, let's appreciate it.

Let us pray, *God, be free to be yourself in my life*. The Almighty. The Holy One. The Savior. The King of the Universe. Lord of Lords. The Suffering Servant. The Lamb that was slain. The Lord our Provider. The Lord our Shepherd. The Lord our Healer. The Lord our Righteousness.

Let's learn to pray. Let's learn to live. Learn to hallow God's name then continue to pray expecting to see God's kingdom come, God's will be done on earth as it is in heaven. This is the promise that carries the broadest reach but needs to find its sharpest focus in each of us.

"Because they will all know me, from the least of them to the greatest." (Hebrews 8: 11b)

"In the last days, God says, I will pour out my Spirit on all people." (Joel 2: 28, Acts 2: 17)

"Arise, shine, for your light has come, and the glory of the LORD rises upon you." (Isaiah 60: 1)

"This is why it is said: 'Wake up, sleeper, rise from the dead, and Christ will shine on you'." (Ephesians 5: 14)

"Look, he is coming with the clouds," and 'every eye will see him, even those who pierced him'; and all peoples on earth 'will mourn because of him'. So shall it be! Amen." (Revelation 1: 7)

We weep as I am sure John Wesley the founder of the Methodist Revival in England did when his heart was 'strangely warmed'. I'm sure his face glistened with tears of joy as he realized Christ had died not only for the sins of the world but for his own. Do you appreciate and recognize the love that Jesus has shown to you. Do you feel his pain as he has felt yours?

This is the revival I pray God will bring – the repentance and faith that gives us the power to rejoice as a nation in the Lord. This is much more and far deeper than consumer confidence. It is not a coerced or forced theocracy. What a sorry excuse for life that would be. When we pray God's will be done we are drawn to reflect on the central verse of the entire Bible: "It is better to take refuge in the LORD than to trust in humans." (Psalm 118: 8) We are not looking for a man, a king, or a charismatic leader to save us or provide for us. That is one of our problems on the right and left. *If we could just elect the right person, one who cares about the average person, or one who was conservative or progressive enough*; the list goes on and on.

God also looks for someone and it's a very frustrating search. "Remember, therefore, what you have received and heard; hold fast, and repent. But if you do not wake up, I will come like a thief, and you will not know at what time I will come to you." (Revelation 3: 3)

Do not wait for the next election cycle. Do not wait for someone else to be in charge. Do not wait for the world to fix itself. The leaders of this world will not call you in for your input. You may offer it but the robotic automated response you receive will tell you all you need to know.

Give Us Today Our Daily Bread

God, on the other hand, is asking for your input. Remember the "Big If"! Keep on praying and trusting in the Lord. Call on him: "give us Lord, our daily bread." God will answer. Remember what the scripture says and doesn't say. It says, "Remember the Sabbath day to keep it holy." It doesn't say remember the 3rd of the month for that is when the check will come. To pray for daily bread is to ask God to prescribe for us what we need each day.

The reverse of this is to continue to self-prescribe our own medication and solution. The end result will be an overdose of self and an accelerated acclimation into sin.

To seek God's provision is to take responsibility for our lives. We don't blame others for our plight. We are not on an endless search for freebies or handouts. We may look for the most economical way of doing things but we are not trying to live off of someone else's dime. We are looking for the ways we can be fruitful and faithful. Do I take advantage of all the assistance I can get? If I am asking for the Lord's provision I have to ask myself is the assistance I am getting honestly received and honestly obtained?

We used to receive an adoption subsidy. Should I have taken it? Yes, I believe I should have. The things we were required to do by the state: counseling, special schools, specialized therapies, the mandated visits and appointments we had to attend would have been financially impossible to fulfill without the accompanying subsidy.

The subsidy received matched the honest needs and obligated care we were expected to provide. I am thankful for it. It enabled us to adopt four beautiful and wonderful children. But asking for God's provision means I will continue to live faithfully after the subsidy is gone.

We plan ahead for rainy days because it rains. We are patient and spend with restraint and forethought because the alternative leads to waste and the terrible want of desire and debt. I have suffered more than I want of "stupid tax", buying something for which I wasn't ready to pay.

As we ask for God's provision for ourselves and our nations we have to set priorities. We lament about sequestration but we have done nothing to stop our wanton and wrongful and wasteful spending. We have idols and redundant habits that rob us of life, liberty, and happiness with God and one another.

We have strained and broken the common bonds of love because we have set our wants and expectation of provision to come from government instead of God. God is self-existent, the living God. Jesus is the resurrected Lord of life. Government is not self-existent. It cannot continue without revenue streaming in from outside itself. Government takes and saps the strength of one to feed another. It will call for trust but the greater force it uses to insure trust will eventually destroy it.

Unless we forsake our addiction to gaining provision outside of God's hands or our own, we will always be someone's slave or dependent. In bondage, however we look at it.

Forgive Us Our Debts, As We Also Have Forgiven

Have you asked your children and grandchildren to forgive you, to forgive our leaders, to forgive us all? We have placed a financial millstone around their neck. Oh, that our guilt could give them gills for breathing underwater where we have put them. Unless we learn how to live by the Lord's Prayer we will continue down our petty and pitiful paths. Will someone tell me why the Department of Homeland Security needs to purchase 1.5 billion rounds of ammunition including 300,000 hollow point rounds, and planning additional purchases of 1.6 billion rounds – enough to shoot every man, woman, boy and girl in America nine or ten times? I've tried to buy a box of 20 cartridges for over a year but they have been out of stock every time I check. The Lord's Prayer calls for us to be forgiven as we forgive. But, I'll be honest; it's difficult to wedge forgiveness into our relationships when we continue to replicate and compact our sin.

By the way, how do you forgive a politician? How do you forgive a representative for failing to uphold and defend the constitution and take common sense steps to right the houses of congress and brings things into order? To pardon or forgive means to set free, not bind a person to where they committed their misdeeds. That would be considered harsh and unusual punishment. We would not punish a bank robber by making him work in one. We would not put an addict in a pharmaceutical laboratory to pay his debt to society?

Nor should we reelect representatives back to their respective offices if during all previous terms they have led or participated in leading the country down a path of fiscal and regulatory suicide. Forgive them and let them represent us in humbler ways by working alongside us at home. There they can be guarded against losing themselves to pride or self-importance.

Our laws and lawmakers were never meant to be skewed scales in any direction (even towards their own districts). A law and a lawmaker must apply to all in equal measure in every place. We must repent of our progressive and regressive ways.

Sometimes when things get really bad the best we can do (and I know this will offend some) is to "come out from them and be separate, says the Lord. Touch no unclean thing, and I will receive you." (2 Corinthians 6: 17) This is not easy. This means if someone has been hurtful to me I may not go to them and expose myself to more pain but I forgive them sincerely from my heart. I do not speak ill of them and I am gracious to them if I encounter them but I don't set myself up or put myself in a position to be hurt again. Forgiveness does not mean I have restored my faith in the one who offended or hurt me. Forgiveness means I choose to demonstrate faith for myself.

Why do we forgive? We forgive because we can. We are free people. We choose to be proper players in the game of life so that means we move from goal to goal. A person who can't forgive is like a runner who can only move from sideline to sideline. That person is not pushing towards the end zone; they are looking for who they can hit as they go out of bounds.

This means if I forgive increasing government debt I best be decreasing my own. If I want people to rely on the Lord then as God's representative, I best be God's hands and feet. If I don't believe government should fund non-essential services and taxes should be lowered then I best be active in working together with others in my community to raise the funds or be productive and charitable enough to cover the needs of my neighbor. If I find that falls short then I will voluntarily in good faith share what I possess to continue to make a difference. This ministry of compassion and forgiveness is given despite knowing whoever forgives the most will be branded as the chief hindrance and trouble maker.

Operate outside of the Lord's Prayer's call to forgive and we will rationalize every sort of oppression. Our way will not have to be subject to reality or fiscal restraints. Reality and restraints will not exist in our world of compassion. We will be generous enough to meet everyone's needs. We may not ever put a dollar into the kitty but our desire to help will be so much more valuable.

But, we forgive all that. We really do. We know forgiveness is more than anyone's intent or hope. We are reconciled to the fact, if the nation does not come to its senses, we will still live and give, laying down our lives for the gospel and for the good of our neighbor. We are fortified in the present because of the cross of Jesus and what he has born for us there but we are certain of the future because of the resurrection.

Lead Us Not Into Temptation

Do we forgive? Do we allow the resurrection to be what convinces us there is life beyond the crosses we are asked to bear? When we pray, 'lead us not into temptation'; is it done so "God can be the one Lord and leader for the course of action we take. We are not justifying ourselves... We are not trying to get even. We do not have the appropriate skill to be masters of the universe."? (p. 95, Moving at the Speed of Grace, Tate Publishing, 2010)

What happens if we try to be masters instead of the Lord's servants? You already know the answer. We go in the wrong direction. We don't forgive. We justify our anger and our impatience. Our prayer life is so puny we can't occupy ourselves two minutes in a check-out line praying for the clerks or the store managers or for our neighbors before and behind us. We ask for the express lane, the easy pass, and the drive through window and we won't them all to ourselves. We want more services and to raise more taxes (if they come from somebody else.) When we pray lead us not into temptation we are asking not for a higher standard but for no standard except our own.

But, when we try to set up our own way and pray 'lead us not into temptation' we will be insisting God bless our way whether it works or not. *God, please don't insist on a standard. Don't tell me your word is authoritative. Don't ask me to choose between my preferences and the conviction of your Spirit. Don't ask me to measure my happiness by your holiness. Suspend the rules for me lest I stump my toe going the wrong way.*

Instead, let us pray "lead me not into that temptation."

Deliver Us from Evil

Admit the obvious and agree with Jesus. Jesus said, "I am the vine; you are the branches. If you remain in me and I in you, you will bear much fruit; apart from me you can do nothing. If you do not remain in me, you are like a branch that is thrown away and withers; such branches are picked up, thrown into the fire and burned." (John 15: 5 – 6) Admit the obvious, starting in the church. We are declining. A Detroit church proclaims, "We are no dry bones." But, if you can't admit you're lifeless, where is the room for God to pour anything new? When are the new wine skins made for new wine going to be used when there is such a dogged determination to never quit using the old wine skins?

If we cannot from start to finish say "I need Jesus to live the life I am meant to live", then deliver me from evil is at best an idle request. At worse, it will become a request for God to leave us out of his kingdom and to remove the gracious influence of his life from ours. Please take this scenario seriously. If we do not hallow the name of God Our Father we are establishing a trajectory for our life that will transform the Good God of heaven into a reference for our own personal evil. If we avoid God like the plaque we have made his ways and commandments to be we will turn ourselves and our nation with all of its glory, honor, and riches over to the devil.

In the parable of the Prodigal Son, the wayward son did a wonderful thing. The Bible says, "He came to his senses". (Luke 15: 17) If we are to have a prayer we will do the same thing.

Study Questions:

1. Do you recite the Lord's Prayer or do you use it as the template for your life and prayers it was intended to be? How do you daily hallow the name of God? Is it the launching pad for everything you are and do?

2. What would be the one thing you could do or stop doing that would elevate the possibility of God's kingdom coming or God's will being done more fully in your life?

3. Thinking on the John Ruskin's quote, "When a man is wrapped up in himself, he makes a pretty small package"; what's one way your life could become a larger gift to the world? To your work? To your family?

4. Read Mark 10: 42 – 45. Now, compare and contrast that lifestyle command by Jesus with the entitlement mentality many hold today. Are we closer to Jesus' way or do we follow a way more like "I do not live to provide for others but to find ways others can provide for me."?

5. Describe what forgiveness does and accomplishes. Did you ever see forgiveness spoken or demonstrated as you grew up? How have you seen it? How have you expressed forgiveness? Can our national debt be forgiven without declaring bankruptcy?

6. In what areas of life as a person and as a nation would it be dangerous for us to be tempted? How can we improve as a nation going forward? What areas of our life require direct intervention from God?

7. When we pray, "deliver us from evil" what in faith are we asking God to do?

What Is The Point?

"Do you think you will escape God's judgment? Or do you show contempt for the riches of his kindness, forbearance and patience, not realizing that God's kindness is intended to lead you to repentance?"
(Romans 2: 3b – 4)

The dream reveals three events: an earthquake in Japan, an earthquake in California, and an impending airplane crash in Eastern Europe. More importantly, there are three questions and three answers that draw us to take action appropriate for what God is doing in the earth. "Why?" I asked. "They honor their dead more than me the living God." Why?" "They claim to be substantial but I will shake them and they will see they are hollow and empty like a drum." "What about us?" "I will deal with you in another way."

Are these the exact words of my dream? They are my best recollection. The letter I sent to myself in April of 1999 sits sealed on my office desk waiting for the fateful 6/22 that was revealed in the dream.

So, what's the point? When the dream first occurred I asked friends for advice on what I should do. Who should I tell? What preparation can be made when you don't know the year? What happens if it's just a vivid dream?

I was advised to seal it up, postmark it, and wait. I did that. The letter is post marked April 16, 1999, Charlotte C.H., VA 23923 and sent to me at my old home address. I have carried this letter with me through four church moves. Sometimes I have been aware of its presence. Sometimes, it has been forgotten amidst the pile of papers I have accumulated. Yet, when I felt the impulse to express God's call in light of the dream, I was led right to the letter. Seeing it, holding it in my hands I was reminded the dream was real. The letter declared the dream was more than a memory. Though the envelope is still sealed, the call of God to us is not.

The call is going out. "The time has come," he (Jesus) said. "The kingdom of God has come near. Repent and believe the good news!" (Mark 1: 15) Now is the time to hallow the name of Jesus. (Matthew 6: 9) Hightail it to God! (Proverbs 3: 5) Rejoice in the Lord. (Philippians 4: 4) Make the Lord your Shepherd. (Psalm 23: 1) Stand when everything is shaken! (Romans 5: 2)

There are two calls God places upon our life but as with everything God does these must be kept in good order. The first and primary call upon our life is to repent and believe; as Paul shares in Romans 8, to live according to God's purpose for our lives. The second call is to be filled with the Spirit of God and in the Spirit's power to serve God and others. I often run across people frustrated trying to develop their life around the second call without deciding for the first.

Putting the second call before the first may work wonders in our self-improvement and in the development of our gifts but it leaves us falling short of eternity. What's the point? Why accomplish great things in the world but leave out what is required of our soul. Jesus tells us to "seek first his kingdom and his righteousness, and all these things will be given to you as well." (Matthew 6: 33) Let's put things in order. Put first things first, second things second.

Bear Bryant is credited with saying, "many have the will to win; few have the will to prepare to win." In light of the dream, I am asking you to have the will to prepare to win. I am asking America if it will turn and make the choice that makes all the difference in the world.

Can this judgment be forestalled? Most of us have heard the story of Nineveh the first time around. Jonah arrived by way of big fish transportation and preached, "Forty more days and Nineveh will be overthrown." (Jonah 3: 4) But, Nineveh wasn't overthrown; at least not in forty days. It was two generations later and Nahum the prophet shares the 'it-is-too-late-for-repentance message'.

Have we sinned away our day of grace? Was Billy Graham our Jonah and now two generations later we are hearing from Nahum? I don't know. We stand on the threshold of making that choice or having it made for us.

What's the point? I believe we can act as if Jonah is still preaching, as if this is a day of repentance, as if judgment can be forestalled. Why do I believe this? It's because of the revival and fellowship I am sharing where I live and serve as pastor. Churches have come together across denominational and racial lines to seek the face of God together. Why do I believe this? It is because I heard a leader say something true. At the first public memorial service after the Boston Marathon Bombing the governor of Massachusetts, Deval Patrick said, "The grace this tragedy exposed is the best of who we are."

This one statement reminds me there is still hope for us in the midst of tragedy and collapse if we let grace rise! If the shaking comes we can make it through if we let grace rise. If the earth shakes and the mountains fall into the sea, I pray we will let grace rise!

I know America deserves judgment. The way of faith that lives by every word that proceeds from the mouth of God has been forsaken. Can it arouse and gain our attention again? Can we find a few righteous souls in our midst to forestall the judgment? Can we stand as righteous souls if it cannot be forestalled? Are their representatives who will risk themselves: their lives, their fortunes, and their sacred honor for the truth? What will we risk for the simple way of grace to rise again?

Do you think Father Abraham is interceding for America as he did for Sodom and Gomorrah and the other cities of the plain? I know Jesus lives to make intercession for us. Will we be responsive to the prayers of Jesus and the saints?

Are there Americans: Christian, non-Christian, believers of every sort who will choose grace and love in the midst of what is coming? Will there be those among us who will support life and liberty? Will there be those who will defy authority to help the weak and to rescue those the world condemns?

Will we be drawn out of our complacent trust of those who lie to us and be raised up as a person who makes a difference with each individual before us? Will we vow not to get sucked into the closed mind of the collective but stand as a responsible person and be one of "those who by persistence in doing good seek glory, honor, and immortality"? (Romans 2: 7) If this describes you there is hope for us all.

We have seen this before: an almost identical situation. Judgment postponed didn't necessarily make life more pleasant. What it did was avert a bloody and destructive fate for a nation who had turned away from God. No, I am not thinking of the Wesleyan revival that spared England the carnage of the French Revolution. I am thinking of much further back in history.

Read the first two chapters of the book of Exodus. There you can follow the unfolding path of sin as it is revealed in the life of a new pharaoh. There you can also follow the movements of grace rising and becoming the means of pushing back judgment and the violent revolution that would have spilled out for another eighty years.

How do we prepare to change the landscape of our nation? Like a good farmer we must turn the ground over. Jeremiah the prophet warns, "Break up your unplowed ground and do not sow among thorns." (Jeremiah 4: 3) Hosea declares, "Sow righteousness for yourselves, reap the fruit of unfailing love, and break up your unplowed ground; for it is time to seek the LORD, until he comes and showers his righteousness on you." (Hosea 10: 12) What was it that turned the ground over in ancient Egypt? It was midwives who feared God more than they feared pharaoh. As Jeremiah describes it, it was someone who would "circumcise" themselves to the Lord. Two beautiful and splendid women set the groundwork for change through their obedience to the Lord.

Now, these were two women who were representatives of the nation and appointed to their work. Despite their official status, despite the available excuse of 'following orders', "they let the boys live." (Exodus 1: 17) They planted the seed of faith that allowed the fruit of the womb to come forth. What areas of our lives can we plant seeds of faith so our children can live despite the edicts of our political leaders? How can we work and conduct ourselves so the work of God can be multiplied?

Who in their official capacity and responsibility will fear the Lord and walk in his ways despite directions to the contrary? Will you join me and pray for spiritual and societal midwives who will bring life giving action to counter the death-leaning choices we are presently following? Let us pray when the crisis of sin and shaking occur it will not be wasted on further acts of control or supposedly emergency measures. Instead, let us choose to stop repeating or adding to the manipulative or criminal choices that put us in a bad place to start.

Let us choose what is right and what is good at its foundation to govern what we do. Let us trust the Lord for blessing and reward. Let us not pick and choose what is appropriate for others and exclude ourselves or play favorites by what we do.

This is similar to what went wrong in Egypt. "Then a new king, who did not know about Joseph, came to power in Egypt." (Exodus 1: 8) Joseph means to add or augment so the scripture implies that this new leader didn't know how to add things up. He betrayed his appointment to office for the one thing required of a leader-to faithfully execute the duties of his office so things add up to more freedom and prosperity for all of the people. Not knowing Joseph also meant he didn't know the man of God that Joseph was so he was leading without the benefit of knowledge or wisdom. He was locked in leading from his own biased way of looking at things. This was further compounded by surrounding himself with people who only reinforced his way of looking at things or in the case of our president having people of different perspectives chosen for your cabinet, but choosing not to speak with them.

The new king's first words recorded in Exodus reveal the walking contradiction he would demonstrate himself to be. "Look," he said to *his* people, "the Israelites have become far too numerous for us. Come, we must deal shrewdly with them or they will become even more numerous and, if war breaks out, will join our enemies, fight against us and leave the country." (Exodus 1: 9 – 10) There's too many of those Israelites but if we don't do something there will be less of them.

Rather than strengthen the bonds of communication and understanding, relationships are weakened and distrust is extended. Rather than work cooperatively, ideas and agendas are pushed through. "So they put slave masters over them to oppress them with forced labor, and they built Pithom and Rameses as store cities for Pharaoh." (Exodus 1: 11) Rather than negotiate, decisions are forced upon the people. Even when bipartisan Egyptian and Israelite projects are completed no credit is given to the Israelites for their help. "But the more they were oppressed, the more they multiplied and spread; so the Egyptians came to dread the Israelites, and worked them ruthlessly." (Exodus 1: 12 – 13)

In fact, any blessing of life not derived from or arising outside of the new king is suspect and must be hindered. Blessing and growth are to be dreaded especially in the wrong places and with the wrong people. Therefore, be it resolved that labor shall be made hard for everybody. The root of bitterness that was first glimpsed in the new king's mandate for change and control now finds its full flower in the bitterness that is painfully redistributed through every sector of the economy and society.

Bitterness gives way to bloodshed. That is the path sin always follows unless repentance comes to decision makers and to those through whom decisions are carried out. Continue along the new king's path and a breaking point of judgment will occur. It may start in inefficiency and waste in one place but eventually it will corrupt the whole and the whole kingdom will be brought down.

What broke the pattern and the outcome of sin? It was the midwives repentance before God. Wait a minute. They didn't follow through with the call to shed innocent blood so from what did they repent? They repented of the new king's program of control as they aligned themselves with the purposes of God. When will the nation and its representatives, its leaders, and its people forego their silence in the face of similar programs of control? When will the church forego its silence? When will the church forego its support of progressive bitterness? When will the church get back its first business: "to evangelize the continent and spread scriptural holiness over these lands?" (The Doctrine and Discipline of the Methodist Episcopal Church, 1892, Hunt & Eaton, NY, p. 3, Episcopal Address) When will the church forego its game of control over the work of the Holy Spirit and return again to the simplicity of God's saving way in Jesus Christ?

If we want to thrive as well as survive the shaking that is coming we will have to repent of being closed to the Holy Spirit. We will have to affirm again there is life giving power in the office of the evangelist that can benefit churches beyond our pastoral ministry. We will have to say of the evangelist and anointed man or woman of God, paraphrasing what the midwives said, "they are more vigorous and give birth" to things our normal pastoral ministry does not. Yes, if we want to live beyond the shaking of our society we will be open to the Holy Spirit and the leading of the Spirit in ways we haven't been before.

We'll address that need again in just a moment but first let's review what we can do to move from being a nation pierced through by following sin's path to a nation who follows the One who was pierced for them. In light of our leadership's inability to add things up, we have to be reliant upon God as Joseph was in his day. Even if we are sold out by our brothers, falsely accused by those we faithfully serve, imprisoned and bound for crimes we didn't commit, forgotten when we give good help, we trust the Lord. We act as God's beautiful and splendid people, midwives of grace and new life.

We sow ourselves to what is faithful and true to God. We entrust our way to God even when it seems it would endanger our life and livelihood.

We watch for what God will do and who God will raise up to choose life and love. We are like Moses' sister waiting in the bulrushes as Pharaoh's daughter saw the basket with her brother inside. "She opened it and saw the baby. He was crying, and she felt sorry for him. 'This is one of the Hebrew babies,' she said." (Exodus 2: 6) Before, compassion and pity can have a second thought Moses' sister is there! "Then his sister asked Pharaoh's daughter, 'Shall I go and get one of the Hebrew women to nurse the baby for you'?" (Exodus 2: 7)

We have to be ready to be 'sister-on-the-spot' when we see people around us respond with love and grace. The new king's daughter knew the law, knew what her daddy had decreed but she didn't share in his betrayal or bloodlust. She had the strength of her own will to choose love and life and Moses' sister was there to reinforce it and cultivate it by providing her a means to continue in the good path she had chosen. "Yes, go," she answered. So the girl went and got the baby's mother. Pharaoh's daughter said to her, 'Take this baby and nurse him for me, and I will pay you.' So the woman took the baby and nursed him." (Exodus 2: 8 – 9)

Are you ready to take responsibility for the moments when those around you make good decisions? Are you there ready to encourage, reinforce, and provide support for those choosing a better path than the one being decreed and mandated from the government? Are you ready to nurse these inclinations along so they can grow?

Finally, are you ready to be drawn out of your comfort zones? Are you and I ready to be named Moses, drawn out of our fears and frustrations to be faithful to God in our day? The Holy Spirit must again be what powers the church and for the truths that are self-evident to guide the nation once more. We can't wait for our leaders to take the lead on this. Moses was just a baby when he received this new name. We may feel just as helpless and as inadequate as a baby to stand against all that is facing us in these days but I know you can be drawn out into being a blessing and a difference maker to those with whom you come in contact. I know you and I can have a repentance that is real, a faith that is made steadfast and a strength that is renewed day by day.

Hard choices are before us. Great problems loom over our nation but I know God gives grace that is greater than all of our sin. Let grace be drawn out to cover a nation pierced and let us be a nation blessed of God again.

Study Questions:

1. In what ways have you responded to the calls of God in your life? Have you decided for the first call of repentance and faith? How are you reinforcing that first call through the call to serve?

2. If we compare America to Nineveh who is our preacher: Jonah or Nahum? Who influences you towards repentance and greater faith? Are pastors, local or nationally known, calling us to repentance?

3. Are our leaders adding things up correctly? How do we pray for our leaders consistently? How can they come to know Joseph and how can they be drawn out of their own biases and places of blame?

4. Where or who are the spiritual midwives in the religious community? In the world of politics? In the media? In the entertainment world? In sports? In the arts? In business? In education?

5. What needs to happen in you for you to be ready to be a sister-on-the-spot, encouraging others to follow up on impulses of love and grace? How do you need encouragement? How do you renew your hope and strength?

6. How do you envision becoming more of a Moses in the days ahead, drawn out of what is comfortable for you into greater faithfulness? Where in your life will the Holy Spirit have greater influence?

A Final Thought

"As God's co-workers we urge you not to receive God's grace in vain. For he says, 'In the time of my favor I heard you, and in the day of salvation I helped you.' I tell you, now is the time of God's favor, now is the day of salvation." (2 Corinthians 6: 1 – 2)

Yes, man has broken the pathway of grace and constructed a hybrid way. This is nothing new. Unfortunately, the scale of our betrayal, the severity of our bias, the substantial way we blame everyone but ourselves for the problems we face will lead to a bitter and bloody breaking point of judgment. Repentance is the only redeeming starting point but most market a faith without repentance in these days.

The prophetic words of Jesus meant to lead us to repentance remind us the last sign of God beginning his final judgment is "earthquakes in various places". (Matthew 24: 7) The shaking revealed in my dream may be the echo and reverberation of God's last call to us as a nation pierced.

Again, I tell you the truth, it is time to turn to Jesus, to Him who was pierced for us. It is time to entrust ourselves to him without reservation, "casting all our cares upon him because he cares for us." (I Peter 5: 7) Just as r comes before s in the alphabet so repentance precedes any solution. Our corruption of soul must embrace its cure before the solutions that can solve our day to day dilemmas are engaged.

This is why I wrote this book. I still hold out hope for the USA but only if we turn from the idols of celebrity leaders, false religions, multiculturalism, socialism, political correctness, greed, and narcissism. Our love of money (ours or somebody else's) and the love of our own viewpoint mar the portrait of grace God is seeking to paint of our lives. For all of us for whom life is an unsolvable puzzle, we must return Jesus to the front of the box and quit the abstract of ourselves we've been using the pieces of our lives to construct.

Even with my limited knowledge I can envision three methods of regaining our footing as a nation and being healed as a land. All must follow repentance or all of these methods will be co-opted and turned against those they were intended to help. Without the great awakening of repentance and revival we will continue to descend into being a banana republic or no republic at all. Our sins will bear the fruit of their own fatal penalty and we will cease to be a "shining city set on a hill" and we will become a byword to the nations, another example of what happens to a people who forsake the way of grace.

These three methods are common ways any of us work our way out of a tight spot. The good news is these methods can be applied to our nation as well as our family.

1. We can sell something. As Dave Ramsey counsels many, "Have a yard sale." Sell something. Almost all of us have junk that others might treasure. Who knows? You won't find out how much you can make until you set it out there.

In 2011, Dr. James H. Boykin, retired Alfred L. Blake Chair in Real Estate at Virginia Commonwealth University set out a solution to our present and future debt crisis in an article titled, "Let's Sell Federal Lands to the Oil Companies". Read it. It was posted April 20, 2011 in the Richmond Times Dispatch. (http://www.timesdispatch.com/news/article_13f5be36-a720-530a-8a36-4c69f629e965.html#.UYY_Y7CKouY.gmail)

I share a couple of paragraphs with you. "Federal ownership of vast, unproductive acreage contributes to our insolvency as well as offers a partial remedy to our government indebtedness and ability for America to gain a measure of energy self-sufficiency. Nearly 30 percent (about 650 million acres) of our national land mass of 2.3 billion acres is in federal lands. Another 8.6 percent is owned by local and state governments. Additionally, there is another 1.76 billion acres of taxpayer-owned lands offshore available for energy production.

Suppose, for instance, that 10 percent of the 650 million acres — 65 million acres — would be offered for sale only to domestic energy companies. Of course, each parcel sold would need to be priced at its respective market value and evaluated so as to weigh its comparative merits for producing energy versus being preserved for environmental or scenic value. For the sake of illustration, if these tracts were sold for an average of $1,500 per acre, the resulting revenue to repay our hemorrhaging national debt would be in the range of $97.5 trillion."

2. We can produce something. I write music and I write books. I do this to share the ministry to which I am called but I also produce these resources to help and benefit others. As I do this, I help and benefit my family and myself, too. When anyone produces, creates, or invents something the benefit redounds to many.

A farmer produces a crop. Their preparation, planting, and cultivation come together to produce a harvest. That harvest is marketed and sold and we rejoice that the benefit of their labor extends to us. Our only concern is that their work will continue into the next season. We don't penalize them for being successful. We give thanks their success will likely mean I can enjoy what they produce at a more affordable rate.

This blessing of production needs to be universally applied for our nation to follow repentance with renewal. God has stayed true to his character and provided us with the means of being blessed. It is our calling to appreciate the gifts of his grace and provision and share them with the world.

In December of 2011 the Institute for Energy Research shared some facts of how blessed we are. "North America is blessed with enough energy supplies to promote and sustain economic growth for many generations. The government's own reports detail this, and Congress was advised of our energy wealth when the Congressional Research Service of the Library of Congress released a report showing that the United States' combined recoverable oil, natural gas, and coal endowment is the largest on Earth."

To sum up their executive summary: "the technically recoverable oil in North America could fuel the present needs in the United States of seven billion barrels per year for around 250 years. Given that U.S. consumption is currently about 24 trillion cubic feet per, there is enough natural gas in North America to last the United States for over 175 years at current rates of consumption. North American recoverable coal could provide enough electricity for the United States for about 500 years at current levels of consumption." (http://www.energyforamerica.org/inventory/)

Producing something means using what we have. As the Institute for Energy Research testifies, we have a lot. What will we do with it?

3. We can release control over things. Not many of us are Harry Houdini. Not many of us can function productively or effectively while shackled. Not many of us can put forth our best effort in a straightjacket. We need freedom to stretch and strive for what is beyond our reach. Life was meant to be a no-handicap race.

Some would argue we have to make things fair. Some have a head start. But, when you handicap a race, making one participant carry more weight than another from start to finish you are making the assumption we are all running the same race.

Are you writing a similar book to this one? If you were would you want me handicapped so we have to publish the same day? Do you really want life to be "fixed" that way? What if your book was ready; would you want to have to wait for me so things could be fair?

What if you feel led to live your life as a sprint to the finish, like William Borden, the millionaire who wanted to be a missionary who died at the age of 25, living his life with "no reserves", "no retreats", and "no regrets"? Or what if you were called to be like…; insert whosever name you wish. The truth is we are called to be ourselves, the unique individuals God called to live according to his purpose whether that purpose takes twenty years or a hundred and twenty.

There is not a single bureaucrat, legislator, president, or group of people able to see our heart, judge our will, or scope out our destiny. It is time to quit pretending that someone can. Only you in a deep and earnest relationship with your Maker can come to that discovery.

It is ludicrous and the height of our sin to think we can govern and handicap three hundred fourteen million races in any given moment or that we can govern the decisions that make up fifteen trillion dollars' worth of transactions each year. It is time for our repentance to be followed by releasing control over some things.

I trust if you have come this far, you have already humbled yourself and are now praying for Jesus to have his way in your life and in our nation. You join with me in praying for one or all of these three methods to be applied to where we are today. We understand the Apostle Paul's words to the disciples of Jesus in Corinth as particularly applicable to us.

> "As God's co-workers we urge you not to receive God's grace in vain. For he says, 'In the time of my favor I heard you, and in the day of salvation I helped you.' I tell you, now is the time of God's favor, now is the day of salvation. We put no stumbling block in anyone's path, so that our ministry will not be discredited. Rather, as servants of God we commend ourselves in every way: in great endurance; in troubles, hardships and distresses; in beatings, imprisonments and riots; in hard work, sleepless nights and hunger; in purity, understanding, patience and kindness; in the Holy Spirit and in sincere love; in truthful speech and in the power of God; with weapons of righteousness in the right hand and in the left; through glory and dishonor, bad report and good report; genuine, yet regarded as impostors; known, yet regarded as unknown; dying, and yet we live on; beaten, and yet not killed; sorrowful, yet always rejoicing; poor, yet making many rich; having nothing, and yet possessing everything. We have spoken

freely to you, *Americans*, and opened wide our hearts to you." (2 Corinthians 6: 1 – 11)

What will we do? Will we love the Lord and turn to Him? Will we get to know Him and find out Jesus loves us and has given himself for us? Will we love our neighbors? Will we get to know them and find out if they love us? Will we humble ourselves to walk with God and each other?

These are the last days for America to stand for life and liberty, and to pursue a daily experience of God's Holy Spirit in our lives. These are the days when we will find out if we will be shaken down as a nation pierced or whether we will be a nation made whole again.

"As for me and my house we will serve the Lord!" What about you?

19730337R00059

Made in the USA
Charleston, SC
09 June 2013